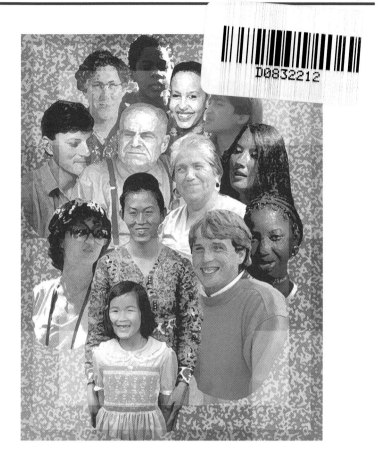

Racial Sobriety:
Becoming the change you want to see

by Clarence Earl Williams, Jr.

Published by the Institute for Recovery from Racisms™
Detroit, Michigan, USA

Table of Contents

This is the second edition of the original work,
Racial Sobriety: A Journey from hurts to healing,
published in 2002.

Dedication

This book is dedicated to the observance of the 500th anniversary of the first African slave to arrive in the western hemisphere on the island of Hispañola, present day Haiti and the Dominican Republic, in 1502. This traumatic event plunged the hemisphere into a living hell for untold millions. This work is dedicated to the struggle of healing this horrendous legacy of racial dysfunction that exists in every republic of this hemisphere.

The book is also dedicated to my parents, Clarence Sr. and Lula Belle, and their parents' parents who entered the American colonies hundreds of years ago and struggled merely to survive as Africans in the America. It is dedicated as well to the White and Nonwhite citizens of this country, particularly the Sisters of the Blessed Sacrament and the Missionaries of the Precious Blood, who have given their lives to advancing the cause of full membership in the human race for every person regardless of race.

Acknowledgments

I would like to acknowledge those who have had a crucial part in developing my approach to racial sobriety. My graduate studies were initiated by the Provincial Director of the Missionaries of the Precious Blood, the Very Reverend Kenneth Pleiman, CPPS. To direct these studies, I turned to a friend who was a former professor, the Reverend Doctor Robert Schreiter, CPPS, who invited me into the doctoral program at Catholic Theological Union in Chicago where he teaches. Under Schreiter's mentoring I explored the contemporary issues in the literature on racism and was directed by Dr. Thomas Nairn, OFM, and Dr. Jamie Phelps, OP. With Schreiter's encouragement, I continued my studies at the Union Institute and University in Cincinnati, Ohio.

My journey at UI & U began with the recommendation to the graduate school by friends who had studied there such as the Rev. Dr. James Goode, OFM, the late Dr. Nathan Jones and the late Archbishop James P. Lyke, OFM, Ph.D. of Atlanta.

My initiation to UI & U was through Drs. Rose Duhon-Sells and Charles Sells in my Entrance Colloquium. Both mentored me throughout my sojourn at the university. I was fortunate to be able to visit with Dr. Sylvia Hill, who served as my Core Faculty member, many times in her home during my time at the university. Her freedom in sharing insights, resources and spiritual energy was a constant source of intellectual development and encouragement. It is due to her responsive mentoring that my work progressed in an orderly, focused and integrated series of new learning events.

The members of my doctoral committee proved to be my "Dream Team" of scholars. Dr. Rose Duhon-Sells served as my Second Core Advisor. Dr. Duhon-Sells shared her years of insights from the vantage point of being the founder of the National Association of Multicultural Educators. Dr. Edwin J. Nichols, an international multicultural and diversity expert based in Washington, DC, had mentored my conceptual development in the cultural dimension of racial conflicts for two decades through keynote addresses for various professional organizations in which I participated. My formal relationship with him in my studies and the critique Dr. Nichols brought to the work were invaluable. Dr. Judith H. Katz joined the committee with her international standing for the last two decades in racial and diversity training throughout the world. I had been using her work for years. The formal relationship of being mentored by her was of great value to my thinking. Two of my peers in the Union Process who served my new learning admirably were Dr. Jeffrey Imber and Jacqueline Haessly. Dr. Jeffrey Imber was a practicing psychotherapist who allowed me to share in his work with a focal group support of interracial men in the Detroit, Michigan area. He also assisted in the development of my approach to recovery from his clinical insights and resources. Haessly, a peace educator, made her unique contribution to the completion of my studies.

My area of specialization was influenced greatly by my global experiences. Adjunct faculty members were very helpful in realizing these new learning experiences. The adjuncts included Rev. Melvin James, SVD, for the Mexico, Brazil and Ecuador field studies; Rev. Felix Mushobozi, CPPS, for the field studies in Tanzania; Rev. James Pawlicki, SVD, for the global internship in Israel, Egypt and Rome; and Dr. Thea Stevenson who mentored me in educational theory and critical pedagogy. All of these wonderfully generous people made my dream program a reality.

During the six year doctoral program journey, I was supported by my staff at St. Anthony Church in Detroit, Michigan. Brother Hugh Henderson, CPPS, the executive administrator of the parish, stepped in to cover events at the parish so as to allow me to give the needed attention to my studies. In 1995, when I joined the

Archdiocese Department of Parish Life as the Director of Black Catholic Ministries, my supervisor, Catherine Wagner, allowed me time to continue my studies. Without the support of my co-ministers throughout these years, the work could not have come to completion.

Technical assistance came from a support team in Detroit, headed up by Alice Liley who went over every draft making the copy corrections. Dug Rusin designed the layout of the book, and created the covers and all the graphics. Brother Terrence Nufer, CPPS, served as copy editor and was assisted by the Rev. Paul Marshall, SM, Emilia Junk and Sama Francis Muma. The proofreading team also included Bruce McDonald, Claudette McMeekins, Phil Barash, Robert Delaney, Herve Glitho, Komlavi Atipoupou, and Zacarias Castigo Buhuro, Karina Hernandez, Jean Noel Fogang and Dn. Michael McKale. Dan McAfee penned the line art. The printing of the book was directed by Dennis Milligan of the Archdiocese of Detroit Printing Office.

Finally, Robert Pawlowicz and Noreen Rossi, MD, gave technical support and affirmation. Support and encouragement came from the National Black Catholic Clergy Caucus which awarded a grant to assist the Institute for Recovery from Racisms™ to promote this book.

A world of people joined me in this project with the hope that it would make a world of difference. I hope they feel their efforts were honored in this work.

How to Use This Book

This book is written for those seeking to move beyond the damaging effects of racism in their lives and our society. The book addresses its audience as good people who are on a journey to become better people in their interracial relationships. The book is also a resource for educators, facilitators, civic and community leaders, corporate diversity trainers and pastoral ministers. It is a tool to share the benefits of the Racial Society™ approach with individuals, small groups, committees, working groups, focal support groups and commissions. An overview of the various uses of the approach can be found on page 173.

The chapters on the Stages of Racial Recovery and Racial Sobriety introduce the reader to the inner complexity and social mapping of our roles as racial actors. The path to racial sobriety leads to a deep encounter with our racialized culture and its impact on our everyday life in society. Each chapter opens with a definition of the stage along with personal testimonies from people who have found their "voice" on the journey towards racial sobriety. The reader is invited to a personal examination of their experience of the various stages of racial recovery and sobriety. The chapters then proceed to describe the dynamics of the stage in the multiple racialized communities in which we live, work and interact. The overview of this treatment of the racialized communities can be seen in the Sociotext. (See pages 202-207.)

Organization

The book is divided into three major sections:

• Overview of the Racial Sobriety and Recovery from Racisms concept, Chapters One and Two.

• Explanation of the Stages of Recovery from Racisms, Chapters Three through Ten.

• Formats and processes for Racial Sobriety, Chapter Eleven.

For the reader who intends to proceed outside of a group process, it is best to read the book from beginning to end. For those who are reading the book in a group process, your facilitator will direct your reading assignments. However, it is beneficial to read the entire work for the best understanding of the process. Besides English, there are materials in Spanish and Portuguese. (See website: www.racialsobriety.org.) Whatever introduction to racial sobriety that your journey might take, it will be enriching and rewarding.

Touring

The resources of this book can be reviewed in various ways depending on the time the reader has available.

• If you have 30 minutes, read Chapter One on Racial Sobriety and the definitions of each stage found at the beginning of each chapter.

• If you have an hour, read Chapter One, the definition and the "Voices" sections of your choice that follow after the definitions in each chapter.

• If you have two hours you could read Chapter One, the definitions, the "Voices"and the "Personal Examination" at the end of the "Voices" section.

• With more time, rsead the entire book to begin your journey to racial sobriety.

More information about how to use this book and further learning opportunities with the Institute for Recovery from Racisms™ can be found on the Internet at www.racialsobriety.org.

Enjoy your racial sobriety!

The Mission of the Institute

The challenge today is to recover the value of each person's humanity in a society where targeted groups are considered less human than others due to their "race." Recovery from Racisms™ is a treatment program to explore the part that individuals and institutions play in the metaracism process that gives energy and support to racial supremacy in our society. The practice of seeing each person as a fully functioning human being in the human family is called "racial sobriety." The work of the Institute for Recovery from Racisms seeks to promote racial sobriety through individual, institutional and cultural transformation.

The Meaning of the Institute for Recovery from Racisms™ Logo

The cross-like figure in the center of the logo is the "ankh," pronounced "awnk". The ankh originated as a symbol of life along the Nile valley over 4,000 years ago. The Egyptian pharaohs were buried with an ankh in their hands to show that they possessed life beyond the grave. For this reason the early Christians of Egypt, in the times of the apostles, adopted the ankh as a sign of everlasting life. The symbol was chosen for the recovery from racisms' logo to represent the new life that racial sobriety offers those who embrace it. When the "stinking thinking" of racisms is eradicated, the flow of healthy thoughts and feelings in action is set free within us.

The ankh stands on a base of two more symbols used in recovery from racisms approach: the triangle of awareness and the Stages of Racial Recovery and Sobriety. The triangle of awareness depicts the three levels of the Racialized Self. (See page 195.) The oval represents the movement through the stages of recovery and sobriety. Together the three symbols represent the goal of becoming fully functional human beings and the treatment program to assist our effort. The logo personifies the good health of mind that allows people to embrace the idea that each person is our brother or sister. Our personal transformation through racial sobriety promotes mental health throughout the human family.

Definition of Racism

Racism is a social illness that is promoted by thinking, feeling and acting as if one race is superior to another race. The origin of racism is in the belief that some people are not fully human, and therefore do not deserve to be treated like full human beings. The full human beings have supreme rights over the less human groups, and therefore have the power of racial supremacy to shape social relationships. In such a social structure members of the dominant culture can harm, segregate and exploit the targeted racial groups. Racism is most commonly used in order to justify exploiting the poor as a group.

To establish a culture of racial supremacy requires the power to control the targeted groups as seen in the conquest of a native population in America (North, Central, South and the Caribbean) or the importation of slaves, or both. Secondly, a culture of racial supremacy needs to control the economic forces that enable it to sustain the dominant group's power over the targeted groups. Thirdly, regulation of social interactions to maintain racial distinction is necessary for ongoing racial supremacy, whether it is enforced by law or observed in social taboos. These laws, formal and informal, try to prevent the mixing of the "races" in social situations. When there is contact, there must be a ritual of how the superior actor and the inferior actor conduct their relationship.

The four elements that provide the means to continually give energy to racial supremacy are: the power to harm, economic exploitation, social segregation and fixed social roles for the targeted racial groups. In time these four elements develop into an invisible culture in the "metaracism" of a society. The term metaracism is used to describe how racism changes its manner and methods from one period of time to another. An example of metaracism is seen in the use of power in regard to racism in the early colonies of America, and today. The power to hurt came after the power to kill and vanquish; the economic exploitation is the after-effect of economic enslavement; and social segregation is the after-effect of the racial caste system of the colonies still present in the U.S. Census. The three elements are at work daily to accomplish the same goal of providing a strategy of racial supremacy for the dominant group over the targeted groups.

Today, we think of racism in terms of White over Black and/or Hispanic/Latino, Native Americans and Asians. However, historically, immigrants from Europe were not considered White for decades after their arrival in this country due to their poverty; such was the experience of the Irish, Germans, Italians and Jews, just to mention a few. Racial supremacy presented, then and now, a valued white status desired by immigrants who came seeking a better life. White racial status gave immigrants in the past and immigrants today a needed avenue to social interaction, economic betterment, and ultimately power in the society.

The dynamics of racial supremacy allow the dominant group to maintain power by giving white status to some and denying it to others. This process is dynamic and ongoing. The most recent example is the 2000 United States Census in which Hispanic/Latinos were asked to identify themselves as "White Hispanic/Latino" or "Black Hispanic/Latino." Since 1970 there has been a Hispanic designation on the census. This reversal in counting the Hispanic/Latino population as another immigrating ethnic group by requesting them to identify themselves in racial groups is a cause for concern throughout our society[1]. Though less than twenty percent choose the Black/White labels, the majority chose "Latino." Some see the new racial categories for Hispanic/Latinos as an attempt to enlarge the "Shrinking White Majority" of the country[2]. Such a movement is an example of metaracism in which the white supremacy culture seeks to offer inclusion into society in exchange for ethnic identity. The ethnicity exchange pressures on past immigrants are revisited as we open the 21st century. The formats for racial identification for Hispanic/Latino population approved for the upcoming 2010 census will continue this metaracism project.[3] It is a clear and strong signal that the white supremacy culture has resolved to make new allies. The result of the 1970 census was a prediction that Hispanic/Latino growth had begun "the Browning of America." The 2010 census is an attempt to see that this population instead becomes the whitening of America.

[1] The American Academy of Arts in 2005 published a series of papers in its journal, Daedalus. Kenneth Prewitt's article, "Racial Classification in America: where do we go from here?", gives a history of the census and the present issues. <u>Daedalus</u> **134** (Winter): 5-17.

[2] Lopez, Ian Haney in <u>Daedalus</u> **134** (Winter): 42-45

[3] Ibid., Prewitt.17.

Voices of Sobriety

Last week, I (White female) was traveling with a colleague (African-American) to a seminar in California. Her airplane tickets had been lost in the mail. We were instructed by the travel agent to report the ticket lost and have the airline reissue a ticket when we checked in at the airport. My colleague completed the paperwork and gave her credit card to the attendant (White female). In a very perturbed fashion and a demeaning tone in her voice, she loudly said: "I am issuing you an E-ticket that you cannot misplace your ticket again." I witnessed she was stereotyping my colleague as an irresponsible Black woman which is done to Nonwhites on many occasions through racial profiling.

I spoke up and said: "Her ticket was lost in the mail. I hope someone does not try to use it." Also, I dropped a note in the mail to the airlines regarding the profiling I observed. I felt good witnessing to my racial sobriety while bringing awareness to an everyday injustice.

— White female

~•~

At the airport in New Jersey I had to catch a cab to Harlem. Because of a winter storm the line for cabs was long and everyone had to double up in order to get a cab. I asked the person arranging cabs to give me a copy with the cost and rights of a person taking a cab. I was far from home and I did not want to be taken advantage of by a driver. When the cab driver (a recent immigrant from his heavy accent) had dropped off the other two Asian passengers, who lived in downtown New York, he told me that he could not go to Harlem. He informed me that he would get another cab for me. I refused the offer and stated that he knew that I was going to Harlem when I entered the cab. Why should I get out in the freezing sleet and get another cab?

The cab driver called the police on his cell phone. Four police cars arrived. I got out of the cab in the freezing sleet and explained to the crowd of police officers what happened. I showed the officers the coupon. The police told the cab driver that, by law, he had to take me to Harlem.

In this situation, I witnessed to my self awareness that Nonwhites are denied their human dignity each day. I "passed on" my witness to the new American cab driver, the police and the crowd that gathered in the sleet to see what the commotion was about. They saw a person able to take the "stinking thinking" of racism and turn the tables. I needed to witness to my racial sobriety. They needed my witness for their understanding that things cannot continue as they are.

— Black male

Respecting Confidentiality:

The personal stories of people struggling with recovery from racisms and racial sobriety that open the various chapters are used with the explicit written permission of each person. The incidents were shared in the Healing Circle process, see page 194. To provide a "safe place to find one's voice of racial sobriety" all things said in the Healing Circle are absolutely confidential. Therefore, these stories are shared through the generosity of each writer.

Chapter 1

What is Racial Sobriety™?

Racial sobriety is a commitment to seeing each person as my brother or sister in the same human family. Racial sobriety requires a self awareness of our interactions with people to examine our prejudices regarding another's racial caste rather than their membership in the human family.

Our global reality requires a new way of seeing ourselves in the world if the human family is to survive. The media broadcasts into our consciousness the assaults of racisms, which are the various ways that people's humanity is denied. The September 11th attack on the United States opened the 21th century to a time of global warefare unseen for decades. This fanned the flame of racial hatred throughout the world. The terrorists became the people to fear. Unfortunately, their cultural and religious background is also targeted as the media speaks of "Islamic terrorists" and "Arab terrorists." What began as a terrorist attack has become a "clash in civilization," the "war against the West." The racial dysfunction has spread from the terrorists to those who hate the terrorists. It becomes harder to see each person as our brother or sister in the global human family of this new century.

Besides the global assaults on the human family, there is the national experience of Hurricane Katrina on August 29, 2005. The lack of effort by the U.S. government to provide relief to its poor and nonwhite citizens in New Orleans, Louisiana, held the world spellbound by the television images. The ongoing hatred for those seen as "the other," in the sense of other than full human beings, is the drama of immigration. In the fear of terrorism, fear of the stranger and finding a social scapegoat, immigrants have come to be targeted as the enemy in our midst. The global, national and local traumas around "racisms" are an assault on the common humanity of every person on the planet. The words of Dr. Martin Luther King, Jr. are prophetic, "We must learn to live together as brothers or perish together as fools."

Racial Sobriety™ is sober thinking, feeling and acting in regard to our race relations. Sober is a word associated with recovery from the abuse of alcohol, drug use and compulsive behaviors. Just as people can "act under the influence" of substances and psychological forces, they also can "live under the influence" of racial dysfunction. The word "sober" is also an acronym for S-O-B-E-R; that is, Seeing Others as Being Entitled to Respect. Thinking, feeling and acting with respect toward everyone is living a lifestyle of racial sobriety™. When we think, feel and act in inappropriate ways, we are under the influence of racial dysfunction, the "stinking thinking" of racisms. The most effective strategy for moving from the "stinking thinking" of racisms is to see each person as a member of the human family. Racial sobriety is a commitment to think of each person as my brother or sister. On the feeling level, we see each person as our brother or sister; on the acting level, we witness to our commitment to see each person as our brother or sister.

To begin the journey to racial sobriety there is a need to know where we are in order to know where we are going. The goal of racial sobriety is to free ourselves of racial dysfunction. The term racial dysfunction describes the negative thinking, feeling and acting on racial difference. In other words, it is dysfunctional to see a person or group as anything other than human beings regardless of their race. Just as for persons who have a dysfunctional use of substances such as alcohol or drugs, and those who have a dysfunctional relationship with eating, work, sex or gambling, there is a need for a treatment program to provide healing for that dysfunctional lifestyle. In the same manner, racial sobriety provides a healing process for our racial dysfunction. The endless racial incidents, reported and unreported, in American society are symptoms of racial dysfunction that arise as Whites and Non-whites respond to the "sick" and "toxic" messages of the culture in which we live. Racial dysfunction is the inappropriate response in thinking, feeling or acting towards another person or people due to their race, culture, language, or religion that denies respect for our common humanity. Racial sobriety is a commitment to rid oneself of the false messages of racial dysfunction in order to become a fully functioning member of the human family who sees each person as a brother and sister in the human family.

Racial Sobriety begins with a recovery process known as Recovery from Racisms™. The recovery stages are presented in Chapter Two. This chapter is focused on the goal itself, Racial Sobriety™, which is the fruit or benefit derived from the recovery journey. The goal of racial sobriety is attained and maintained through re-engagement, forgiveness and witness. Re-engagement is a stage in which a commitment is made to racially sober thinking and acting. Life changes begin within oneself and one's relationship with others. Because racial sobriety affects every aspect of one's life, each person will re-engage in their own unique way. Chapters Eight through Ten offer a fuller examination of the three stages of racial sobriety.

One of the great human beings of the 20th century was Mohandas K. (Mahatma) Gandhi (1869-1948), the human rights leader of India. Gandhi said, "You must be the change that you want to see in the world." As we free ourselves from the "stinking thinking" of racisms, our racial sobriety allows us to "be the change that we want to see...". Thus, the title of this second edition, ***Racial Sobriety: Becoming the change you want to see.*** The first edition was entitled, ***Racial Sobriety: A journey from hurts to healing***. Gandhi inspired the thoughts of Dr. Martin Luther King, Jr. (1929-1968), the great civil rights leader of the United States. As we enter the 21st century the work of healing the human family of its racial dysfunction continues. Racial sobriety is an approach that embraces the wisdom of discovering change within our own personal transformation, and extending that transformation through every thought and action we perform. The lives and legacies of Gandhi, King and Mother Teresa of Calcutta (1910-1997) bear witness to the power that racially sober people can have as leaders. As we embrace racial sobriety, we become the change that we want to see.

To maintain racial sobriety amid a world of racial dysfunction, the exercise of forgiveness builds strength for the journey. The first step is to forgive ourselves for "going along to get along" in a racialized culture. Most people live a life of accommodation to the white supremacy culture. As we forgive ourselves, we become more understanding of others and the power that racial dysfunction has over their lives. This sense of compassion assists us in forgiving others. Each act of forgiveness takes the toxic power of anger, resentment and hostility and transforms it into new energy that supports our journey to racial sobriety.

The Witness stage is the ultimate goal of racial sobriety. Witnessing is passing our racial sobriety onto others. Becoming the change we want to see empowers us with self-esteem, confidence and wisdom. Our witness is personal, and our sharing will reflect our personality and circumstance. Our very presence is a form of witness. Personal sobriety benefits our mental health, social enjoyment, spiritual renewal and everyone around us. The transformation within the racially sober person also extends into their social interactions and has the power to transform the world. As more people come to embrace racial sobriety, we become members of the Human Family that sees each person as our brother or sister.

Witnessing also calls for a public face that demonstrates to others that racial dysfunction hurts everyone in the human family, not just the Nonwhites who are victimized by it. Racism takes something away from every person on the planet everyday. It is through witnessing, privately and publicly, that we come to maintain our own racial sobriety. The impact of our public witness becomes the foundation upon which to build a culture of racial sobriety in a world of racial dysfunction.

Racial sobriety involves visiting the three stages of re-engagement, forgiveness and witness in order to grow in strength, wisdom and freedom in regards to the racial dysfunctions in our lives. As each person embraces racial sobriety, their presence is felt as a new member in the New Family Formation process. New Family Formation means that as each person embraces racial sobriety they leave behind their racial caste allegiance to join the human family in which each person is seen as my brother or sister.

A Language for Racial Sobriety

To describe the unique approach of racial sobriety, a number of terms, both familiar and unfamiliar, have been selected. The reader is invited to see these terms anew from the perspective of racial sobriety. These terms assist us to take a sober look at the reality in which we live and to recognize the racial dysfunction throughout the culture. When using terms that apply to "people" such as White, Nonwhite, Black, Asian, Native American, Hispanic/Latino, Intermediates, Colorist, etc., capital letters are used. However when using terms that apply to "things" such as whiteness, nonwhiteness, white privilege and white supremacy culture, they will appear without capitalization. The following explanations will shed more light on some of the terms mentioned.

The Nation/Family

The nation/family is a description for seeing each country as a unique blend of people who depend on one another for their life, quality of life and culture. Our lives begin as citizens in the context of our family and extend to social institutions which take on the parental role for the culture. The concept of the nation/family describes how the family and nation both share in the formation of the person's racial identity. The task of racial sobriety is to intervene in the racial dysfunction of the nation/family in such a way that healing begins. Recovery from racisms is to restore to the nation/family its proper relationship with all of its citizens by overcoming the dysfunction of racism. The social illness[1] of racism denies full participation of everyone in the human family.

The Racialized Self and
the Racial Caste Hierarchy

To intervene in racial dysfunction, let us consider the racial reality in the world in which we live. When reflecting on our particular race in the white supremacy culture, it is seen through the lens of the "racialized self." (See page 195.) The racialized self is a description of the racial identity that a person is given in their society in order to facilitate the racial caste hierarchy. The construction and managing of the racial caste hierarchy is an ongoing effort. N. Brent Kennedy in his book *The Melungeons: The Resurrection of a Proud People,* notes that in the first United States census in the 1790's there were four available categories in the racial castes of the emerging republic: White, Indian, Negro and Mulatto. The term "mulatto" came to be used for those who seemed White but were not pure White. While the reality of sorting out human beings by skin color challenged clear classifications, what remained certain was that white status would be the summit.

"...*many census takers—including the registrar of vital statistics for Virginia well into the 1940's—would arbitrarily divide people into but two races: "white," which meant only "pure" northern Europeans, or "black," which meant blacks, mulattos, Indians, Jews, Arabs, Asians, and so forth, or anyone with as much as one-sixteenth so-called "nonwhite" (that is, non-Anglo) blood."* [2]

The racialized self is the center of one's racial identity. Racial identity is formed by the community of origin of the person and is used to direct their social interaction with others within and outside of that racial community. Racial sobriety sees racial dysfunction as the product of the negative thoughts and feelings from racial socialization. Through intervention in the "stinking thinking" processes of racism the collusion with the white supremacy culture is challenged. Ultimately, racial sobriety ends the sickness of racial dysfunction in a person's life.

Each racial description holds a history of a peoples location in the racial caste hierarchy. The present racial caste order is being challenged today due to the new immigrants. For the racial order to continue to exist there need to be cultural forces that will reorganize the racial caste hierarchy by determining what races will be the in-groups and out-groups. At this time the United States census again is taking the parental role in the nation/family as the institution to maintain the historical racial descriptions. Racial dysfunction in the nation/family results in the inability to exist in social harmony outside a fixed racial hierarchy. The racial caste hierarchy works against racial sobriety for any of the members of its society whether White or Nonwhite. Those with white privileges do not want to give them up. Those without these privileges do not want to live without them.

"People of Color," referred to in this book as Nonwhites, have physical differences from European Whites. When these physical differences are classified as indicators of different races, they can be used to exclude equal treatment between the racial groups. As Lieberson notes in *A Piece of The Pie*:

Let us recognize at the outset that there are certain disadvantages that blacks and any other nonwhite group would suffer in a society where the dominant white population has a preference for white over nonwhites. This disadvantage is one blacks share with Japanese, Chinese, Filipinos, American Indians, and any other nonwhite group. These groups were more visible and more sharply discriminated against than were various white ethnic groups.[3]

The pre-existing racial caste hierarchy educates through hard lessons the saying: "If you are White, you're all right. If you are yellow, you're mellow. If you're brown, stick around. If you are black, get back." Historically, some Native Americans and Blacks have tried to pass as Whites for social mobility.[4] Today, some Hispanics/Latinos[5] and Asians[6] can be observed attempting the same strategies as these groups struggle with the forces of racial dysfunction in the racial castes.

In light of the different communities of origin and their multiple expressions of racial dysfunction, the focus of this work is not on racism as a single phenomenon, but on *racisms* as the multiple responses to race which are expressed in a white supremacy culture. These racisms are produced as part of each community's (White, Nonwhite, Intermediate and Colorist) historical response to the culture in which they live.

White Supremacy Culture

The term white supremacy culture is a description of the social and political order that places power in the hands of those designated as "White" in a society. The intellectual foundations of white supremacy in the West are evident in two of the most celebrated European philosophers of the Enlightenment, David Hume and Georg Friedrich Hegel.[7] White supremacists created the fiction of "races" to give a rationale for the conquest, genocide, human slavery and the domination of the Nonwhite world. They argued the inferiority of the African and other Nonwhites to the "white race" in order to serve the ends of the business elite of their day and today. Due to the systematic education and development of culture in the Western hemisphere racism impacts and informs every social interaction. The reality of racism is throughout the human community. The global experience of racism was the topic of the 2001 United Nations meeting in Johannesburg, South Africa entitled, "World Conference Against Racism." As a social illness racism is pandemic in the global community.

Historically,White designates a racial category for those members of society on whom have been conferred this sociopolitical status by the U.S. government since the time of slavery. Though slavery as an institution was abolished after the Civil War, racial domination of Nonwhites continued with the establishment of "Jim Crow" laws in the South and the North.[8] Many European immigrants, such as the Germans, the Irish, the Italians, the Jews who arrived after 1830, were not Anglo-Saxon Protestants, and were not considered White for many years.[9] Today as the United States experiences the greatest number of immigrants in its history, some immigrants are conferred White status and others, particularly Hispanics, are not yet classified as such. Hispanics, Latinos and Asians in this model would be considered as Nonwhite, not as it pertains to the color of skin, but in terms of their racial caste by the United States census. The terms White and Nonwhite are conferred on the basis of the ideology of privilege rather than the idea of color of skin.

White supremacy is an ideology that has the power to confer privileges on those members who have "White" status and to make outcasts of those members who do not possess it. White supremacy is a result of historical acts, specifically the conquest and genocide of the indigenous native populations and the enslavement of various African people by some of the conquistadors and colonizers of America. Present day institutional networks maintain the hegemonic processes of white supremacy beyond a specific color, class or country. It goes beyond such groupings as today's "skinheads," the Klu Klux Klan and neo-Nazi groups.[10] The Center for New Community, a Chicago based organization that monitors hate groups, released a study a few months after the September 11, 2001 attacks noting the rise of "white collar" racism among the White middle class against Jews and immigrants. "The report identified 338 white nationalist groups in 10 Midwestern states: Illinois, Indiana, Iowa, Kansas, Michigan, Minnesota, Missouri, Nebraska, Ohio and Wisconsin."[11] The cultural forces that began in colonial America with the framers of the Constitution are with us to this day. Their presence bears witness to the support of a cultural will and institutions to maintain the status quo of privileges for Whites as it disenfranchises Nonwhites.

Ruth Frankenberg challenges the notion that racial language divides people rather than unites them in her book *White Women, Race Matters: The Social Construction of Whiteness*. Language makes visible what is invisible.

Naming "whiteness" displaces it from the unmarked, unnamed status that is itself an effect of its dominance. Among the effects on white people both of race privilege and of the dominance of whiteness are their seeming normativity, their structured invisibility. ... To speak of whiteness is, I think, to assign everyone a place in relation of racism. It is to emphasize that dealing with racism is not merely an option for white people-that, rather, racism shapes white people's lives and identities in a way that is inseparable from other facets of daily life." [12]

White and whiteness

Nonwhite and White are terms used to describe the two major groups that in this book reflect the racial caste hierarchy. The use of these two terms highlights the way the white supremacy culture organizes its life in the various countries of this hemisphere. Peter McLaren, an educator, emphasizes the importance of the term White for a better worldview of social and global interactions.

...unless we give white students a sense of their own identity as an emergent ethnicity—we naturalize whiteness as a cultural marker against which otherness is defined..."whiteness" does not exist outside of culture but constitutes the prevailing social texts in which social norms are made and remade..."whiteness" has become the invisible norm for how the dominant culture measures its own worth and civility.[13]

The centrality of "whiteness" in understanding racial supremacy is the cornerstone of many writers who address race as central to American politics in everyday life.[14] Use of the terms "White" and "Nonwhite" constitute a shift in the "cultural gaze"[15] of the conversation on race. This emerging conversation is called Critical White Studies. People of Color are no longer the problem to be addressed when discussing the race issue. On the contrary, the white supremacy culture is the problem to be studied and the center of the race issue. The term "White" makes the "invisible" population that generates much of the racism "visible" to be examined and analyzed rather than the Nonwhite victims of white supremacy.[16]

"What is 'whiteness,' or a 'White' person?" is an often heard question in discussions of race. Patti DeRosa describes the term "white" as having three elements.[17]

As a description, whiteness identifies those who are light-skinned, with Western European physical features. As a physical description, this label is fairly self-evident. The experience of whiteness in the United States is one of unearned privileges which all white people receive in various ways due to racism. A light-skinned "white" person who experiences race privileges may or may not buy into the ideology of whiteness as a system of exploitation based on white supremacy. However, that person can not separate her/himself from the experience of being white, since we live and breathe the privileges every day.

The term "white" is used throughout the book in relationship to the three elements of "whiteness," that is, White as a racial description, as the experience of enjoying white status and political sense of white privilege in social interactions.

Everyday Racisms

The use of the term "everyday" is used throughout the book to speak to the fact that racism is not limited to "institutional racism" or civil rights but focuses on the role of racism in the life of every person on the planet whether White or Nonwhite. Philemina Essed speaks to this reality in her book, *Understanding Everyday Racism.*

Once we recognize the fact that racism is systemically integrated into meanings and routine practices by which social relations are reproduced, it follows that it is not specific agents but the very fabric of the social system that must be problematized. This requires that we reformulate the problem of racism as an everyday problem. This analysis of everyday racism makes it clear that racism must be combated through culture as well as through other structural relations in the system.[19]

The impact of racism is hidden in the culture and revealed in incidents. However, to provide a healing of the hurts, a treatment will involve an approach that understands the cultural nature in which the racial acts take place. Racial sobriety focuses on the individual's self awareness of their "everyday" collusion with the white supremacy culture or their collaboration with New Family Formation.

Enfranchisement as Social Healing

The political aspect of white privilege is described by the term enfranchisement. This enfranchisement means that through white privilege the avenues of social advancement are open to those individuals and groups with white status. Enfranchisement is the glue that holds the white supremacy culture together. Enfranchisement as used in the recovery perspective describes membership in a social, political and economic community. Full membership includes avenues to employment, education, political determination and status/prestige. Disenfranchisement is the state of being excluded from the avenues reserved for the enfranchised community. This disenfranchised community becomes the minority, those living on the margins of the empowered community. Their numbers might be greater than the enfranchised community but they have less power to determine the outcome of their lives.

The term, "Nonwhite", describes the opposite reality from the term White in relationship to enfranchisement. The nonwhite population are those for whom enfranchisement has been denied based on their racial description, their racial experience and their political position as outcasts in the white supremacy context. Therefore, White and Nonwhite are terms with a larger meaning than solely the description of skin color.

Finally, racial sobriety must move beyond the personal recovery from dysfunction to the transformation of society and its cultural life. The social dimension of racial sobriety is to end one's collusion in maintaining white supremacy through social, political and economic arrangements. Collusion is defined as private or public actions to disenfranchise a person or a people from their participation in the nation/family's resources: employment, education, politics and social recognition. The racialized identity of each person becomes an instrument for collusion with the white supremacy culture against Nonwhite members. Nonwhites also collude with the while supremacy culture as they compete within society against other ethnic groups. And, sadly, Nonwhites and Whites collude within their groups to gain advantage by trying to be "whiter" than one another. These symptoms of racial dysfunction are captured in sayings such as: "They are my color but not my kind." "If you are yellow, you are mellow. If you are brown, stick around. If you are black, get back." There are also other terms such as "white trash." The racial dysfunctions that are produced in the racial castes of American culture are endless.

Racial sobriety is a journey that can begin with the individual alone or with companions who are seeking to make the healing journey. Whether alone or with others racial sobriety is a commitment to self awareness and intervention in one's racial dysfunction within oneself and one's world. This book is meant to assist the individual and the group to become more self aware and effective in treating their racial dysfunction in such a way that their healing journeys transform the culture.

The vision of the New Family is realized through the stages of racial sobriety: re-engagement, forgiveness and witness. These stages sustain the healing process for individuals and groups in their racial dysfunction. The reader is invited to become a member in the New Family and to pass on the benefits of racial sobriety - seeing every person as their sister or brother.

1 The term "social illness" captures the meaning of racism as an affliction affecting the whole society. The author encountered this term while visiting St. Ignatius Church in Philadelphia, Pennsylvania. During a service, a prayer was offered for those affected by 'social illnesses.' Darling Villena-Mata's *Walking Between Winds: A Passage Through Societal Trauma and Its Healing* captures the origins and impact of social illness.

2   Kennedy, N.B. (1997). *The Melungeons: The Resurrection of a Proud People. Macon, Georgia:* Mercer University Press. P.12-13.

3   Lieberson, S. (1980). *A Piece of The Pie: Blacks and White Immigrants Since 1880.* Berkley, CA, University of California Press. 366.

4   Russell, K., M. Wilson, et al. (1992). *The Color Complex: The Politics of Skin Color Among African Americans.* New York, Harcourt Brace Jovanovich.

5   Rodriguez, R. (1982). *Hunger of Memory: The Education of Richard Rodriguez, An Autobiography.* New York, Bantam Windstone.

6   Lee, J. (1997). *Performing Asian America: Race and Ethnicity on the Contemporary Stage.* Philadelphia, Temple University Press.

7   *Review of Emmanuel Chukwudi Eze's book Race and the Enlightenment: A Reader* (Cambridge, Mass.: Blackwell Publishers, 1997) as published in the Journal of Blacks in Higher Education, Summer 1997, 137-8.

8   Davis, F. J. (1993). *Who is Black?: One Nation's Definition.* Pennsylvania: State University.

9   Ignatiev, N. and J. Garvey, Eds. (1996). *Race Traitor.* New York, Routledge Publishers.

10   Novick, M. (1995). *White Lies White Power: The Fight Against White Supremacy and Reactionary Violence.* Monroe, ME, Common Courage Press.

11   Stearns, M. "White supremacists turn white collar." Knight Ridder News Service. Published November 18, 2001. Internet. November 18, 2001. Available by http://www.pioneerplanet.com/news/nat_docs/184677.htm.

12   Frankenberg, R. (1993). *White Women, Race Matters: The Social Construction of Whiteness.* Minneapolis, University of Minnesota Press.7.
Fine, M. et al., Ed. (1997). *Off White: Readings on Race, Power and Society.* New York, Routledge. 6416

13   McLaren, P. (1989). *On Ideology and Education: Critical Pedgagoy and the Cultural Politics of Resistance. Critical Pedagogy, the State, and Cultural Struggle.* H. A. Giroux and P. McLaren. Albany, NY, State University of New York Press. 107-8.

14   Winant, H. (1997). "Behind Blues Eyes: Whiteness and Contemporary U.S. Racial Politics". *Off White: Readings on Race, Power and Society.* Ed. M. Fine. New York, Routledge. 49.

15   Fine, M. et al., Ed. (1997). *Off White: Readings on Race, Power and Society.* New York, Routledge. 64.

16   Wray, M. and A. Newitz, Eds. (1997). *White Trash: Race and Class in America.* New York, Routledge. 3.

17   Fine, M. et al., Ed. (1997). *Off White: Readings on Race, Power and Society.* New York, Routledge.; Frankenberg, R. (1993). *White Women, Race Matters: The Social Construction of Whiteness.* Minneapolis, University of Minnesota Press.; Essed, P. (1991). *Understanding Everyday Racism: An Interdisciplinary Theory.* Newbury Park, CA, Sage Publications.; hooks, b. (1996). *Killing Rage: Ending Racism.* New York, Henry Holt and Company Inc.

18   Thompson, B. (1997). "Home/Work: Antiracism Activism and the Meaning of Whiteness". *Off White: Readings on Race, Power, and Society.* Ed. M. Fine. New York, Routledge. 357.

19   Essed, P. (1991). *Understanding Everyday Racism: An Interdisciplinary Theory.* Newbury Park, CA: Sage Publications. 295.

20   Turner, J. H., R. J. Singleton, et al. (1990). *Oppression: A Socio-History of Black - White Relations in America.* Chicago, Nelson-Hall. 2.

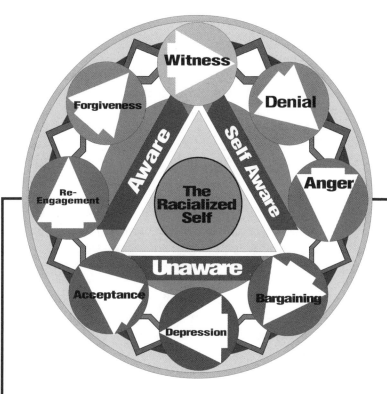

Stages of Recovery and Racial Sobriety™

Voices of Recovery

September 11, 2001 afforded renewed opportunities for racial profiling and scapegoating by White Americans towards People of Color, especially those from the Middle East and South Asia. To keep my commitment to racial sobriety I took part in a three-day event entitled "Rededication to Justice." The event centered around June 23, 2002, as the twentieth anniversary of the brutal and racially motivated murder of Vincent Chin in Highland Park, Michigan. The attackers thought he was Japanese and linked him to the rise of Japanese auto sales in the U.S. Vincent Chin was Chinese American and was in the bar celebrating his bachelor's party like any other American with his friends. The conference days included the award winning movie "Who Killed Vincent Chin?" and ended with an interfaith memorial service held at Forest Lawn Cemetery at Vincent Chin's gravesite.

In my re-engagement, the murder of Vincent Chin brought me to the awareness that there are many people who superficially view other persons, (i.e., their physical structure and features) never taking the time or making the effort to understand them as persons. "These people who look alike" are stereotyped and scapegoated.

— Asian female

~•~

Our ancestors were the "mestizaje" (the mixing) of the Spanish conquistadors and the indigenous people they conquered. To this day, it can be heard (and I've been guilty of this myself) when you see a baby, if he/she is light skinned, the exclamation is usually, "Aye que bonito nino/bonita nina" (oh what a beautiful boy/girl). However, if the child is dark skinned almost invariably you'll hear, "Hay pobrecito/pobrecita; esta prietito/prietita" (oh, poor child, he/she is so dark). By and large we still equate beauty with whiteness.

– Hispanic/Latino male

Chapter Two

What is
Recovery from Racisms™?

Recovery from Racisms™ is a treatment program to "intervene" in racial dysfunction and promote racial sobriety. The nature of intervention in recovery from racisms lies in its pursuit of racial sobriety in which the individual, the group and the culture are challenged to examine the false and sick beliefs of the racialized self. The five stages of the treatment program are borrowed from Dr. Elisabeth Kubler-Ross' work with terminally ill patients which was presented in her famous book *On Death and Dying*. In a similar way the persons seeking racial sobriety are challenged to die to their racialized social identity in order to embrace New Family Formation in which they see each person as their brother or sister.

The five stages of intervention for the racialized self which come from the "death and dying" model are: denial, anger, bargaining, depression and acceptance. Recovery from racisms involves a "death" to the sick thinking, feeling and acting of the racialized self in one's personal and social life. The author came to adopt this approach due to the successful adaptation of the Kubler-Ross model by Dennis and Matthew Linn in their book *Healing Life's Hurts: Healing Memories through the Five Stages of Forgiveness*. Their borrowing of the "death and dying" model addressed the healing of painful emotional traumas in life through a five stage process. Beginning with the Kubler-Ross' "death and dying" model and following the lead of the Linn brothers' "healing life's hurts" the author presents a theory and program for recovering from racisms. See page 189 for an illustration of the models used in the construction of the recovery from racisms approach.

The aim of the recovery process is not only to "die" to the sick thinking, feeling and acting out of racial dysfunction but to go beyond dying in order to live as a member of the New Family through racial sobriety. As explored in Chapter One, the last three stages of recovery are stages for racial sobriety: re-engagement, forgiveness and witness. These stages are necessary to provide a road to "living" as a racially sober person. Recovery from racisms becomes a process of dying to racial dysfunction in order to give life to racial sobriety. This personal racial sobriety requires two elements to treat the social illness of racism commitment and self awareness. One's personal pursuit of racial sobriety makes every social interaction an occasion for promoting healthy racial interactions. The influence of racism in the culture makes so many social interactions full of sickness in thoughts, emotions and acts. The effect of one's racial sobriety on the transformation of our social networks can be seen in the beneficial responses from others.

Racism as a Sickness

How do we treat the sickness of racism? Think of the gains in science against various diseases. For thousands of years the human family died from unseen germs, viruses and bacteria. Once humanity could understand the reality of these unseen forces, health and long life followed. For humanity to take its next giant step in global health, the unseen forces in the diseases of human relations must be understood for the prevention of social illnesses. Racial dysfunction is the major social illness that is toxic to everyone in the world today. Racial dysfunction describes the sick thoughts, feelings and actions that demonstrate the belief in a racial caste hierarchy of superior and inferior races. Racism, like any other disease, is a deadly force in the human family. Its influence threatens the survival of the human family. Recovery from Racisms™ offers a New Family Formation process as a treatment for personal and social health. It presents the Stages of Recovery as a prescription for a chronic condition in the human family for those who seek to journey from hurts to healing through racial sobriety.

To be a member of the New Family requires a racial sobriety which sees each person on the planet as a brother or sister. Maintaining and witnessing to racial sobriety is the cure because it allows the individual to see each person as a human being, not as the "other." This does not mean a blindness to the beauty of humanity's hues. As the late Dr. Frederick Sampson of Detroit said, "Don't be color blind. But don't let color blind you." See the humanity of each person which goes beyond their hue-manity. The color of a person's skin becomes a trigger for racial dysfunction in people who are affected by the disease of racial dysfunction. The vision of the New Family challenges the sick condition of our racially dysfunctional family. The New Family is a metaphor, model or paradigm – a way of describing one reality by comparing it with a more known reality. The New Family metaphor and paradigm speaks to the ability to see the human family relationship over and above a racial caste relationship. The transformed experience of a healed human family is like an injured limb of the body restored to proper use. The idea of recovery from racisms supports healing as the goal of race relations. It is a common vision shared by many writers and activists in antiracism efforts.

Racial Healing

The challenge of leadership in the area of race and ethnic relations is, "How do we begin the healing process?" "How do we begin to make the human family whole once again?" To grasp the problem of racism and racial dysfunction most leaders use metaphors, models and paradigms to describe the work that needs to be undertaken. As the twenty-first century opens, there are many authors who use the comparison or metaphor of "racism as a disease" in the social body. This metaphor can be seen in the titles of some of the latest works to appear on racism which include: *Healing in America: A Prescription for the Disease* by Nathan Rutstein and *Racial Healing: Confronting the Fear Between Blacks & Whites* by Harlon Dalton. Some works relating to racism use the metaphor of racism as a "disease of the mind" in such titles as: *Race: How Blacks and Whites Think and Feel about the American Obsession* by Studs Terkel, *The Rage of a*

Privileged Class by Ellis Cose, *Killing Rage* by bell hooks and the classic *Black Rage* by William Grier and Price Cobbs. When writers use the metaphor of "racism as a disease" and locate the racism in the body, racism is often referred to as a cancer.[1] "Racism as a disease" is also used as a metaphor with addiction such as alcoholism or substance abuse.[2]

There are a number of voices that use this metaphor of recovery from addiction to talk about treatment for racism. Clergymen such as the late Archbishop James P. Lyke, OFM, Ph.D., have proposed a 12-step program approach for the treatment of racism. No matter where one's metaphor places racism, whether in the social body, the mind, or the combination of body-mind, the effects of racism are characterized by pain. This pain includes the pain realized in oppression, fear of the oppressors, sick and toxic social interaction, and civic unrest.

Recovery from Racisms™'s Paradigm for Healing

The metaphor of healing racisms through recovery suggests that Recovery from Racisms™ might be a 12-step program similar to those used by persons recovering from alcoholism and drug addiction. Recovery from Racisms shares some of the features of other recovery programs, but not all. In this book recovery is used as the metaphor and the paradigm for healing. However, it is not used to address substance abuse or process abuse but abuse in the human family's relationship with one another. Racisms are the abuse of persons based on the "stinking thinking" that one group is superior to another group, and worst of all, acting on those thoughts. The "stinking thinking" of racism is referred to as racial dysfunction. Racial dysfunction describes the sick behaviors of the racialized self. The symptoms of racial dysfunction can be seen in those actions that represent a belief in a racial caste hierarchy in both the White and Nonwhite communities. Racial dysfunction can also describe the negative thinking and acting towards people who are regarded as less than human because they differ in race, ethnicity, culture or religion. Recovery from racisms is a treatment program to bring to light how racial dysfunction operates in the life of people throughout the society in which we live and in the world at large.

There is certainly a need for a Psychotherapy for the Public Interest [3] that approaches our racisms as a sign of a deep nation/family dysfunction. As in the case of an individual seeking treatment from a dysfunctional family or community of origin, recovering from racisms in our white supremacy culture will take a similar intervention. The intervention will have to occur in both a psychological formation and a New Family formation. The importance of this dual treatment is seen in the work of the Caribbean psychiatrist, Dr. Franz Fanon. He was raised on the Caribbean island of Martinique, studied in Paris and worked in Algeria, North Africa. Fanon wrote extensively on the psychological ravages of racism in two of his books, *The Wretched of the Earth* and *Black Skin, White Mask*. Here Fanon presents the role of the family in the formation of mental illness.

It can never be sufficiently emphasized that psychoanalysis sets as its task the understanding of given behavior patterns within the specific group represented by the family. When the problem is a neurosis experience by an adult, the analyst's task is to uncover in the new psychic structure an analogy with certain infantile elements, a repetition, a duplication of conflicts that owe their origin to the essence of the family constellation. In every case the analyst clings to the concept of the family as a "psychic circumstance and object." [4]

In approaching recovery from racisms the United States is viewed as a nation/family. The family is a metaphor for American society and its history of psychosocial interaction. The implication of this metaphor is that everyone in this society is affected by the racial identity formation process of their respective communities of origin, White and Nonwhite alike. Because of this family and community socialization, a racial caste hierarchy is generally understood by all citizens reaching adulthood in their societies. The dysfunction of racisms permeates the individual's inner life and social interactions. As a result we are a nation that needs to recover from our family dysfunction of racisms. Nonwhites (People of Color), though the victims of racism, are also in need of recovery from their codependent position in a white supremacy culture that has surrounded and shaped their various communities' histories and their destinies. Whites are in need of recovery from their community of origin formation, educational processes and media bias that have instilled in them negative racial concepts, feelings and behaviors towards Nonwhites.

Collusion and Cultural Healing

A powerful dynamic that begins in the family and is present in the extended nation/family are the "Don't Rules." These "Don't Rules" are found in families where there is abuse and in abusive relationships in general. The social collusion of the denial and bargaining stages represents a cultural pattern in the American family's response to social trauma. Darling Villena-Mata in her book *Walking Between Winds: A Passage Through Societal Trauma and Its Healing,* describes the many responses abused groups develop to protect themselves. She points out a significant defense mechanism that supports cultural denial known as "Don't Rules"[5] which were developed by Claudia Black, Janet Woititz and others.

The Don't Rules are "don't feel, don't trust, and don't talk." In other words, do not feel your feelings, do not trust yourself (or others), and do not talk about it-the problem-to others...[6]

The "Don't Rules" allow for social interaction to continue as if nothing terrible is happening in the family, the relationship or the nation in terms of the abuse being suffered and witnessed. These abuses could be personal or social. The Don't Rules are in force for the individuals in families as well as people and groups abused by social arrangements in regards to race, gender or sexual preference. (See page 190.) Given the widespread experience of people living with the "Don't Rules", it is not surprising that in the American nation/family the military tries to resolve its problems dealing with the presence of gays and lesbians with a policy that says "Don't ask, don't tell." It is in this cultural denial of trauma and efforts to bargain that the recovery from racisms process takes its cue.

In the recovery from racisms process the rules become: do

talk to others, do feel your emotions and do trust yourself. The stages of recovery is a process that requires the dropping of the "Don't Rules" in our society and embracing the "Do Rules." For example, the denial stage requires that one thinks about their collusion with the racial dysfunction of their culture. Anger is a stage to examine what our racial dysfunction does when it is confronted with a situation. A trust of one's judgment is called upon in the bargaining stage to determine how collusion is present in a situation. The depression stage calls for exploring the feeling of powerlessness and loss that racial dysfunction can bring to bear in one's emotional life. And the challenge of the acceptance stage is to trust the knowledge gained in our personal inventory in order to make a commitment to racial sobriety.

The Don't Rules of the dysfunctional nation/family and their support of the racialized self can be seen in the Racial History Journal entries beginning each chapter. These entries represent people embracing the Do Rules of racial sobriety. They invite the reader to identify with the struggle to be a fully functioning[7] human being in a world of everyday racial dysfunction.

For the Don't Rules to be effective every member of the family must cooperate. They must turn a blind eye to the subject in order to act as if nothing is happening. Racial dysfunction is maintained in the silence of not talking, in the numbness of denying feelings and in the anxiety of not trusting oneself and others. Historically, it has been the denial in the culture that has challenged the advancement of the healing of the American nation/family's racial dysfunction. This means both the denial of the dignity of the human person and the denial that turns a blind eye to this reality.

Acting to cover up the abuse in the family is collusion. The word "collusion" in the recovery process describes the act of turning a blind eye to racial dysfunction in order "to go along to get along" in one's family, organization or society. In the recovery from racisms, collusion is playing along with the white supremacy culture in order to be a part of society and advance one's status (social, economic, political). In essence, recovery from racisms is intervening in one's collusion with the power that white supremacy culture holds over one's life.

The Racialized Self and Awareness

Intervention in the process of collusion can occur on the three levels of knowing in an individual: the unaware level, the aware level and the self-aware level, (see page 195). To collude with the nation/family dysfunction of racisms it is necessary to understand the reality of the racialized self. The idea of "race" is a fiction, a make-believe concept. Today the science of DNA demonstrates that everyone in the world has a common ancestor in the human races' first parents in Africa. There is one human race, not races. The racialized self, therefore, is a fiction. But this false belief becomes a fact of life in the real incidents of racial dysfunction. The fact is that many people act on the belief that there are superior and inferior races rather than one human race. As we live in a world infected by this false belief in the mind, heart and soul of our civilizations we suffer its horrific symptoms daily from a "fiction lived as a fact."

Most people are unaware of their racialized self because the white supremacy cultures in which they live follow the Don't Rules of avoiding even the thought of race. However, this state of unawareness comes up to the level of conscious awareness when one comes in contact with a person believed to be of another race. When people actually give themselves permission to reflect on their thinking, feeling and acting this experience moves to the level of self-awareness. They become self-aware of their racialized self with its messages from the culture, its feelings of the heart and the role they are to act out in the relationship with the racialized "other."

The great majority of people are governed by the "Don't think," "Don't feel" and "Don't trust" rules. Another Don't Rule is that of not accepting responsibility for what one comes to realize when reflecting on the insight gained from a racial encounter. To escape responsibility there is the act of "scapegoating," that is, blaming someone else for the problem. Often this is an attempt to defend oneself against feeling obliged to take some action. Scapegoating takes away personal responsibility to make a difference and leaves the person using this response with a sense of social innocence in regard to the racial encounter.

To arrive at being a person who has embraced racial sobriety the journey begins with intervening in the collusion of the racialized self. Abandoning the Don't Rules becomes the act of beginning one's journey to becoming a fully functioning human being and a member of the New Family. We become members of the New Family when we overcome the false belief of the racialized self and rediscover the reality of one human family and the unity of humankind. In the New Family formation we see each person as our brother or sister.

Eight Stages vs. Twelve Steps

The recovery approach of racial dysfunction differs from the popular 12-step programs not only in its focus on family dysfunction but also in the stages of the recovery process. As the 12-step program moves to restore sobriety from substance and process abuse the Recovery from Racisms™ process has 8 stages which restore not only the person but the human race to sobriety.

The stages of racial sobriety are found in other traditional support group processes in which the recovering person is responsible to "pass it on." The three stages of passing on racial sobriety are: Re-engagement, Forgiveness and Witness. Re-engagement is the key to racial sobriety as we take up our lives with the quest for seeing each person as our brother or sister. Forgiveness is an important process of ridding oneself of toxic anger, resentment and bitterness. Finally, witness is the act of passing on the benefits of the sober self and the healing process to others.[8] These three additional stages are the author's constructions that come from field research in Africa, South America, Europe and throughout the United States.

The end of recovery is more than intervening on the racialized self. It is restoring the self to proper functioning by re-engaging attitudes and behaviors with the energies that were used in racial dysfunction. Like other recovery processes there is not an end to recovery but a "road."[9] It is a journey from the hurtful racialized self to the healed self, from family dysfunction to proper functioning in the human family.

Racial sobriety represents the mountain top experience of recovery from racisms. The stages of intervention provide a map for the climb or a compass for the sea. In the midst of the sea of racial dysfunctions the stages are our compass to guide us to solid ground.

The following chapters will continue your introduction to racial sobriety beginning with its five stages of intervention (denial, anger, bargaining, depression and acceptance), and continuing with the three stages of racial sobriety (re-engagement, forgiveness and witness). The chapters will identify the symptoms of racial dysfunction in the human family as seen in the United States.

At the time of publication of this edition the U.S. population had reached 300 million. Forty years ago, in 1967, the population was 200 million and the Civil Rights movement was underway. Unnoticed at the time, an unprecedented wave of new immigrants was gradually arriving. The country had closed its borders to large numbers of immigrants since the early 1920's to allow the last wave of European immigrants, mostly Catholic, to become part of the "melting pot." Unfortunately, the melting pot metaphor worked for "Whites only." The huge population of immigrants, along with the historically nonwhite races (Negroes, Coloreds, Indians and Orientals), are not seen as members of the American family/nation. Our society is in need of a healing process for racial dysfunction of the American family/nation. As we embrace the healing journey of racial sobriety, we become the change we want to see.

1 Sontag, S. (1977/1978). *Illness as Metaphor.* New York Review of Books *"NYREV, Inc."* Part 1: vol. 24; Part 2 /3 vol. 25**:** Part 1: 10-16 ; Part 2: 27-29; Part 3: 29-33; and, Feagin, J. E. and H. Vera (1995). *White Racism: The Basics.* New York: Routledge.

2 O'Connell, N. J. (1990). Racism Sapping Vitality of Church. *The Priest.* 46: 18-21.;   Schaef, A. W. (1987). *When Society Becomes an Addict.* San Francisco: Harper & Row Publishers.

3 Lerner, M. (1987). *Public-interest psychotherapy: A Cure for the Pain of Powerlessness in Surplus Powerlessness.* Utne Reader.

4 Fanon, F. (1967). *Black Skin, White Mask.* New York: Grove Press.; (1963) *The Wretched of the Earth.* New York: Grove Press, Inc.

5 Villena-Mata, D. (2002). The "Don't Rules" in Societal Trauma and Its Healing. *Nonviolent Change Journal.* Vol. XVI, No. 3 Spring, 2002. Download from http://home.earthlink.net/~circlepoint/narticle0100.html on 4/17/02.

6 Ibid.

7 The phrase "fully functioning human being" comes from the work of the late Dr. Thea Bowman, a religious nun who taught theology and race relations throughout the U.S. from the 60's to the 90's.

8 Beattie, M. (1989). *Beyond Codependency: And Getting Better All the Time.* Center City, MN: Hazeldon Book.

9 Peck, M.S. (1998) . *The Road Less Traveled.* New York: Simon & Schuster. 11

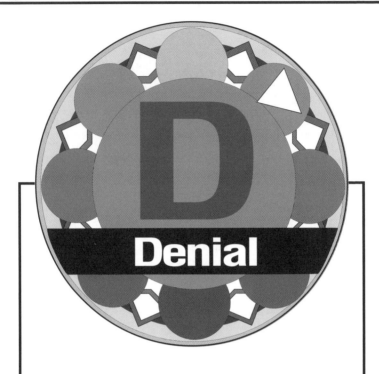

Denial

Denial is a two-edged sword of avoidance and attack. One edge of the sword is used to avoid dealing with racism by turning a blind eye to its reality. The second edge of denial is the act of attacking the humanity of a person or a people. It begins by making a group "the other," "those people" or through demonizing the group. Denial is the act of avoiding and/or attacking a people's from full membership in the human family.

Voices of Denial

I feel uncomfortable when I am with friends and relatives within my white community of culture whenever a discussion arises regarding the number of black families moving into the neighborhood. Reminded of the white flight of the city in the 70s, the discussion will focus on the potential of increased crime and the potential devaluation of property when "those black people" move in. Many times I would remain silent allowing them to continue with their unjust accusations thus colluding with their feelings of superiority and "stinking thinking."

Therefore, through my silence I am denying the fact that I am part of this community of white privilege that has prevented people of color from acquiring good jobs, nice homes and good education. In the future, I need to be part of the solution rather than continuing to enable white elitist attitudes.

– White female

~ • ~

Several years ago at the "Day of Reflection" during a presentation on "The History of Racism in the United States and the impact on the People of African Descent" I started to cry. I felt my whole being shaken to the core. The pain in my heart was one of immense sorrow and I wasn't quite sure why. At the time all I knew was that I had a deep feeling of sadness which overwhelmed me and I could not shake it off for quite a while afterward.

It was not until I began working on my racial sobriety that I realized why that day was so painful. I was in denial about my collusion with the "white supremacy culture" – "going along to get along." I pretended on many occasions during my life that everything was alright because it really hadn't affected me. I was in total denial. I am a fifty-eight year old African American woman who is proud of her heritage now but it took me a long time to accept my ancestry. It took the "Day of Reflection" and my road to racial sobriety to realize how deep rooted the impact of my collusion had affected me and those around me. I thank God for giving me the strength and opportunity to take this road.

– Black female

~ • ~

As a newcomer (immigrant) from Nigeria in West Africa, who had lived and worked in the United Kingdom, I came to the United States of America believing that I can easily get a befitting job.

I applied for different jobs in the white suburbs of Metropolitan Detroit, precisely 20 different companies. Though I knew I was qualified, I never got past the interviews. I thought I was doing something wrong, this brought me into denial. I did not realize that I was being discriminated against. I discussed the issue with one of my professors, who arranged some in-school interviews for me and I did very well. I had blamed my failure on myself rather than the white interviewers.

– Black immigrant male

~ • ~

A few years ago a member of a social justice committee asked me to join the newly established group. I gave the person several excuses as to why I could not be a member. Nevertheless people kept insisting so I weakened and agreed to be a member. I heard myself telling others constantly how I do not want to be part of this committee because I had too much work already. And in addition to that I don't like giving workshops, etc.

I see my refusal to join as the act of denying my past encounters with racism. These encounters were too painful and hurtful to reflect upon. I do not want to surface past hurts and preferred to ignore the entire issue of racism in my personal and community life.

– Nonwhite Hispanic/Latina female

~ • ~

About 12 years ago I was working on a housing rehabilitation construction crew in Trenton, NJ. The foreman of the whole job at that time was White but the crew leader was African American. I recall one day hearing the crew leader relate a story to the foreman about how he was harassed by the police in Princeton while simply driving the van through the business district. I recall thinking to my self that he, the crew leader, was probably not telling the whole truth. I had seen this individual before in behaviors I considered irresponsible. I therefore assumed he was not relating to the foreman the "real" reason the cops had pulled him over.

I see this as denial because I was denying the double standard used by police. It was not my experience that the cops stopped White people without a legitimate reason so I denied the racist intent of the police to harass African Americans in order to persuade them from coming into the business district.

– White male

Personal Examination

Unaware

When facing a situation that raises racial issues do I try to ignore it by avoiding the thoughts and feelings?

Aware

Do I recognize in myself the desire not to be aware of certain racial issues?

Self Aware

How does my denial benefit me? How does it harm me?

Introduction to Denial

When people do not wish to face an unpleasant reality or an emotional shock they often make use of the defense mechanism of denial. It can be an automatic and even a necessary reaction that provides an emotional space to come up with a solution to a challenging situation. Reactions can range from emotional stress to psychological breakdowns. There are more than 100 defense mechanisms that have been observed by psychologists. In pursuing racial sobriety denial is the initial obstacle to the recovery from racisms process.

Though denial is the first stage that is examined an understanding of its dynamics is important because denial is the backdrop for the other stages of anger, bargaining, depression and acceptance. The stages are like pearls on a string with denial as the clasp that holds them together.

The denial found in individuals reflects the denial that surrounds them in a white supremacy culture. Culturally, there is a range of manifestations from the casual denial of racial issues to the racial crisis when denial gives way to anger and breakdowns in the social order. The breakdown in society indicates a crisis that needs to be faced. Until a person, family, community, institution or nation is ready to address the "stinking thinking" of racial dysfunction they are in a state of denial. Denial is a two edged sword. One edge of denial is used to avoid dealing with racism by turning a blind eye to its reality. The second edge of denial is the act of attacking the humanity of a person or a people. It begins by making a group "the other," "those people" or through demonizing the group. Denial is the act of avoiding and/or attacking a people's full membership in the human family.

Denial as a psychological mechanism protects the person, group and/or culture from facing problems that they would otherwise overwhelm their ability to cope in their usual ways. However, the use of denial in racial dysfunction is not an issue of protection from being overwhelmed by reality but the avoidance of responsibility for them. This use of denial allows citizens to carry on their pursuits free of social responsibility and the resulting guilty feelings for failing them. Denial of participation in a white supremacy culture is a form of collusion against the Nonwhite members of society by both Whites and Nonwhites. The term collusion is used here to describe the act of "going along to get along" with others in spite of the social evil that is the result of one's active cooperation and/or passive silence and acceptance.

"Going along to get along" is an accepted form of denying an individual's responsibility for the actions going on around them. This detachment from racial issues is rewarded on many levels in a white supremacy culture through access to better opportunities for the individual and their families. When the code of collusion or other racial taboos is broken the punishment for Whites and Nonwhites ranges from social rejection to death.

The everyday personal use of denial can be viewed as a protection from the feeling of anxiety when racial issues arise. The Rev. Dr. Boniface Hardin, OSB, describes racial anxiety as a "FIG complex." In the FIG complex people often experience fear, ignorance and guilt during a discussion on racism. (See page 190).

People have fear of what might happen to them in such a discussion. They also feel ignorant in terms of how to speak about race (multiculturalism, diversity, ethnicity, nationality) or the terms to respectfully call people (Black/African American, Indian/Native American, Asian/Oriental, Mexican/Hispanic/Latino, White/Caucasian/EuroAmerican). The guilt feelings arise from the realization that they are not as open to others or that they are not as knowledgeable as they should be on these matters. The FIG complex increases the anxiety level because people become more fearful that their ignorance and guilt might be discovered in various interracial encounters. This fear of discovery negatively conditions their openness to these random encounters and/or planned discussions. It is also an obstacle to their learning about the nature of the problem and its solutions. Everyday denial is used to keep racial issues from surfacing so as to protect us from negative emotions of the FIG complex. However, when we can break one of the legs upon which our racial anxiety is supported we can break the spiraling cycle of the FIG complex. The collapse of the FIG complex releases us from the prison of racial anxiety and we no longer need the protection of our denial mechanism.

Our anxiety concerning racial issues becomes an emotional resource that gives fuel to the ongoing collusion supporting the white supremacy culture. This use of everyday denial keeps us from recovery from our racial dysfunctions. This form of everyday denial makes us an ally to the social collusion going on around us.

This chapter examines the dynamics of denial in a white supremacy culture. In looking at the stages of intervention in racial recovery in American society five communities of origin are presented to demonstrate how the dynamics of the stages unfold in the various groups. The two principal racial communities that will be examined are the White community and the Nonwhite community. There is a further division within these two principal communities that make up the Sociotext for Recovery from Racisms. (See page 200.) The subgroups of the White community are the White supremacist community and the White interracialist community. The subgroups of the Nonwhite community are the Nonwhite interracialist community, the Nonwhite supremacy community and the Intermediate/Colorist community. The five designated communities have been singled out to represent the most common currents of observable behaviors with regard to race that are in American society. They are not the only communities in the country in regard to these behaviors, but they would include the largest number. Most Americans in our nation/family find their origins in one of these communities.

Besides denial as a way to deal with the anxiety of race in our society the term is used throughout this work to denote an attack on one's humanity. The process of constructing the racial caste hierarchy in this hemisphere is the cultural result of the denial of the full humanity of untold millions of people. Historically, the act of denial was initiated as a core belief of white supremacy with the first encounter between Europeans and the native people of the United States as well as the other republics in this hemisphere.[1] The denial of the humanity of the native people began with the "demonization" of this group by the conquistadors and the business leaders in search of labor.

Against the backdrop of Christian supremacy in religion the native people were seen as demons. Christian understanding considered those who were not members of the Holy Church as less than full members of humanity and the state. As other immigrant groups arrived from Europe the business, government and church powers provided reasons to justify the stealing of lands from the original inhabitants by denying that the American Indians were fully human due to differences in religion and culture. The Europeans thought of themselves as civilized and the Chosen People of God, as many White supremacists believe today.[2] In this model the indigenous people of the America were the biblical Canaanites of the Promised Land who were destined to be conquered and killed by the Chosen People of God.[3]

The white supremacy notion of civilization placed the European people at the summit of humanity and the American Indians as a lower form of persons on the scale of civilized humanity. In this argument the native peoples of the America were divinely sentenced to be ruled by Europeans whether from Spain, Portugal, France or England.

The act of denial of Nonwhites' humanity was adopted in Anglo America as part of the United States cultural heritage. These sentiments were captured in the political and military agenda against the native peoples called "Manifest Destiny" at the end of the nineteenth century. Horsman noted the historical meaning of "Manifest Destiny".

And as Anglo-Saxons (the United States) sought out the most distant corners of the globe, they could ultimately replace a variety of inferior races. The Anglo-Saxonism of the last half of the century was no benign expansionism, though it used the rhetoric of redemption, for it assumed that one race was destined to lead, others to serve—one race to flourish, many to die. The world was to be transformed not by the strength of better ideas but by the power of a superior race.[4]

This belief of the business class of South America became the dysfunctional racial core belief in the social education of immigrating Spaniards. This model of social organization in the New World was adopted by the business class of the other European colonizers of South America and the Caribbean. In the United States, the same dynamic of race relations was adopted from the Latin American experiment of the conquest of native people and the importation of Africans as slaves. This adoption brought with it the necessity of inviting Europeans to enjoy the rich bounty of the New World in exchange for a securing white supremacy of the European population. These immigrants would become the agents to advance the white supremacy cultural doctrine from the Eastern seaboard to the shores of California and from the Great Lakes to the Gulf of Mexico. This racial dysfunction was instilled into the racial identity formation of every person in the society: the ruling Anglo White elite, the Native American, the African slave and the newly arrived European immigrant. Just as earlier inhabitants were socialized into a racial caste system which was under construction, succeeding generations would be born into the caste system and live out their lives in the context of these insane social relationships.

The denial of the Native Americans' membership in the human race prepared the cultural mind set for another horrific entrepreneurial act, the importation of millions of African people into the hemisphere as slave laborers.[5] The previous racial dysfunction of the nation/families throughout the hemisphere allowed the denial of personhood to extend to Africans as also being Nonwhites in relation to Whites.

The church as a white social institution provided a theology for white supremacy and preached this to all the members of the society, both White and Nonwhite. The religious justification was that slave labor was in exchange for being saved from a savage and godless state of life. It was also taught that the obedient and productive slave would be rewarded in the after-life for their services to Whites while on earth.

From its colonial origin, the core belief of racial dysfunction stands on the denial of the humanity of the Nonwhite person.

European immigrants were educated and socialized into these dysfunctional social arrangements of the white supremacy culture over Nonwhites. The term "Nonwhites" refers to those who where considered so at the time such as Indians, Africans, Mexicans and Orientals. Later, it was also used to refer to other ethnic groups not considered "White" such as the Germans, the Irish, the Italians, the Jews, the Poles, the Hungarians, etc. It is through denial that Whites and Nonwhites alike become desensitized to the plight of Nonwhites. The normal healthy feelings that make for a well ordered society are focused toward those who are White and the same feelings are denied to those who do not have white status. To be treated like a fellow human being is reserved for "Whites only." The denial of a person's humanity can be a "two way street." It can also work as "reverse racism" in nonwhite supremacy which is a mirror image of white supremacy.

Collusion with the existing social order makes it easy for both Whites and Nonwhites to deny the reality of any responsibility for racial dysfunction while attempting to enjoy the privileges reserved for those with white status. "White privilege" includes living without the realization that part of the privilege is to live without any responsibility for racism or having to admit that one benefits from racism. In the urban centers of the United States white privilege was and is protected through segregated neighborhoods and housing covenants that keep Nonwhites from having access to stable communities with better property values, policing and schools. The people within the White community enjoy their privileges based on this exclusionary process that daily maintains an urban apartheid across the nation. In rural America cities and towns had laws that would not allow Nonwhites to be on their streets after dark or stay overnight in any home. These rural communities supported the white supremacy culture by creating their own sense of white privilege. Their social collusion with the white supremacy culture was a demonstration of their solidarity with other "good, decent White people."

Today urban, suburban and rural communities often note their lack of racial diversity but fail to acknowledge that this is the result of the enforcement of segregation. These communities are a testament to the bumper stickers that read "You Are White Today Because Your Parents Practiced Segregation."

The benefits of whiteness so influenced many European immigrants that they chose whiteness over their previous ethnic identifications which labeled them as Nonwhites. They were surrounded by cruel incentives for such a striving. They observed other Nonwhites being subject to indignities and chronic atrocities that held millions of people continually at risk for horrific treatment if they did not keep their place in the social apartheid of Indian reservations, segregated ghettos and barrios. Where there was contact with the white society Nonwhites usually were expected to act as social inferiors and to respond with a sense of gratitude in their service to their social superiors.

Historically, immigrating groups had to struggle to attain white status through social collusion. The attainment of white status was motivated by the social and economic benefits that whiteness offered for themselves and their children. Today, the same strivings and strategies can be observed with contemporary immigrants who are African, Arab, Asian, Eastern European and Hispanic/Latino.

In summary, society's white supremacy culture is the result of the historical denial of the humanity of Nonwhite people in the various republics of the Western hemisphere. The denial of the humanity of native people throughout America (North, South, Central and the Caribbean) is seen in the campaigns of genocide against them in the past and present day. The motto often repeated in American western movies "the only good Indian is a dead one," speaks to the racial dysfunction that was and is still present and promoted in various parts of the hemisphere.

The second great cultural denial was that of the humanity of the Africans as demonstrated by the slave trade and the enforced labor of millions of Africans who built the republics of this hemisphere. Despite the 500 year presence of people of African descent Blacks continue to occupy the lowest rungs on the economic, social and political ladders throughout the Western republics.

Finally, there is the ongoing cultural demand directed towards new immigrants to deny their ethnic and national identities in order to fill the slots in the racial caste hierarchy of American society. In the denial of their previous cultural and national identities, these immigrants bring new energies to the existing racial castes and its resulting racial conflicts. In the process of populating the nation some new immigrants collude with the white supremacy culture while others confront the white supremacy culture as they are assigned to the low rungs of the racial caste hierarchy. Today in the United States the large Hispanic/Latino population is one of the groups at the center of this process which forces immigrating people to choose a "race card" to play in the social interactions and the political life that surrounds them. The United States Census is encouraging these new immigrants to choose between being "White Hispanic/Latino" or "Nonwhite Hispanic/Latino."

The ongoing oppression of Nonwhite persons in America continues in every republic of this hemisphere. Each generation for the last 500 years has experienced the pain and horrors of supporting white supremacy in their respective societies. Due to this experience all the republics of this hemisphere suffer greatly from their racial dysfunctions which are their cultural legacy of racism. In order to begin the healing journey of the American nation/family this generation is challenged to intervene in its denial of supporting and benefitting from racism. We are challenged to make this intervention because our personal denial allows social forces to continue to deny the humanity of our brothers and sisters.

In previous generations the culture desensitized White citizens to the plight of Nonwhites with an appeal to reason and religion which provided the justification needed for the theft of lands and exploitation of slave labor. The cultural denial of the humanity of Nonwhites took away the guilt of the average White and Nonwhite citizen by placing the responsibility on civil laws and religious justifications produced by the intellectual and moral leaders. However, today new leadership is uncovering the roots of racial dysfunction in our cultures.

Discussions and conversations concerning the American nation/family's taboo areas of racial history are becoming commonplace in the news coverage, political discourse, academic research due to the drive for multiculturalism in education and diversity in the workplace. Such conversations can begin to move the nation/family from its historical hurts to the necessary healing that is needed in the life of every member of our society. In the academic world, there is a growing movement in a new field called "Critical White Studies." Critical White Studies seeks to uncover the history of the process by which European immigrants became "White." Examples of the emergence of this new field of study are books such as *How the Irish Became White* by Noel Ignatiev, *Whiteness of a Different Color: European Immigrants and the Alchemy of Race* by Matthew Frye Jacobson and *How the Jews Became White Folks: and What That Says about Race in America* by Karen Brokin. These efforts to tell the nation/family's story provide an understanding of the journey of immigrating Europeans who began to populate certain roles in the racial caste hierarchy.

Freeing society from the grips of our cultural heritage and freeing the racialized self are the challenges of every generation of Americans –it is the challenge of this generation also. The work of recovery from racial dysfunction begins with overcoming denial. The two faces of denial are the two places for our work: from the inside out and from the outside in. Both the White and Nonwhite communities are challenged to embrace this work. From the inside out, recovery from racisms intervenes in order to free us from our denial that blinds us to our reality. In the pursuit of social innocence we deny how involved we are in the evil in our world. Stanley Hauerwas, an educator on morality and ethics, speaks of the idea of presuming that we are good simply because we pay attention only to the good things going on around us.

"...how goodness can become deeply corrupted by its innocence... most of the time innocence is deeply immoral because it is such a lie not to acknowledge that we live in a very complex world that we benefit from, and we don't have to acknowledge the havoc our benefits depend upon.[6]*"*

As we work to recognize the racisms in our culture and ourselves we are challenged to move beyond denial.

Besides the inner work, there is the work to be done outside in our social settings. Recovery from racisms requires us to discontinue any act that would deny another person's humanity. Without racial sobriety we degrade our own humanity in the denial process. Without intervention in our racial dysfunction we degrade those around us by denying their humanity as well.

Dr. Joel Kovel, a psychiatrist, speaks to the ongoing cultural process of denial when he notes: *"(racism is) the systematic exclusion of another from humanity, based superficially upon his color or ethnic origins, and profoundly upon one's own participation in a historical process that degrades him[7]"*.

As citizens we live in the context of the larger culture and we experience its various forms of racisms. Our everyday experience in our white supremacy culture demonstrates the need for racial sobriety whether we are White or Nonwhite. Our generation can accept the challenge to engage in recovery from racial dysfunctions which "degrade" us all. We have the power to become the change we want to see.

1 Talbot, S. (1981). *Roots of Oppression: The American Indian Question.* New York: International Publishers.; Bigelow, B., Ed. (1992). Interview with Chief Tayac: Struggles Unite Native Peoples. Rethinking Columbus: Teaching About the 500th Anniversary of Columbus Arrival in America. Milwaukee, WI, Rethinking Schools.; Nash, G. B. (1992). *Red, White, and Black: The Peoples of Early North America.* Englewood Cliffs, NJ, Prentice Hall.; Kromkowski, J. A., Ed. (1994). *Race and Ethnic Relations 94/95. The Annual Editions Series.* Guilford, CT, The Dushkin Publishing Group, Inc.

2 Ridgeway, J.(1990). *Blood in the Face: The Ku Klux Klan, Aryan Nations, Nazi Skinheads, and the Rise of a New White Culture.* New York: Thunder's Mouth Press.

3 Nash, G. (1992). *Red, White & Black: The Peoples of Early North America.* Englewood Cliffs, New Jersey: Prentice Hall.

4 Horsman, R. (1981). *Race and Manifest Destiny: The Origins of American Racial Anglo-Saxonism.* Cambridge, MA, Harvard University Press. 303.

5 Harris, J. E., Ed. (1993). *Global Dimensions of the African Diaspora.* Washington, DC: Howard University Press.

6 O'Neill, P. (2002). "Theologian's feisty faith challenges status quo." "National Catholic Reporter". Kansas City: Cover Story.

7 Kovel, J. (1970). *White Racism: A Psychohistory.* New York: Pantheon Books. 231.

Denial in the White Response
to White Supremacy Culture

White Supremacist Denial: Denial that Nonwhites are
members of the human family, my brothers and sisters

The 1990s produced books, articles, news reports and film documentaries on the rise and growth of White supremacist groups. White supremacist groups include such names as the Ku Klux Klan, United Klans of America, White Patriot Party, the Invisible Empire, White Aryan Resistance, Nazi Skinheads, Posse Comitatus, Aryan Nations, etc.[1] The actions of White supremacist groups center on celebration of their whiteness in such expressions as, "It is simple that to be born WHITE is an honor and a privilege." But their actions are also against the Nonwhites and White Interracialists with whom they want to avoid contact at best, agitate race war against or worst. Lately, their collective efforts have been to foment race war and establish "a new white only homeland" in the Pacific Northwest of the United States.[2]

Much of the effort of the White supremacist to deny the humanity of Nonwhite people is not the work of terrorist groups but of professional people working in the mainstream of society and in respected organizations. Robert Miles, a famous contemporary White supremacist and theologian of White supremacy, rose to national prominence in Detroit, Michigan. He is the example of an outstanding member of society suffering with racial dysfunction.

Mind, I was at one time the finance chairman of the Republican Party in this state. I was the editor of the American Society of Safety Engineers Newsletter. I was president of the Insurance Executives Society. I was an accepted member of the establishment. I wasn't stupid enough to think I could wear a white robe while I attended their meetings. I know there was a line, and there was going to be a price to pay.[3]

In Miles' words not all White supremacists "wear a white robe" but their influence and power are felt throughout the society at every level of activity to ensure and support a white supremacy culture. To maintain such a culture they simply need others "to go along to get along."

Though most readers will not come from a White Supremacist community of origin, it would be difficult to say that we do not participate in cultural denial.

White Interracialist Denial: Denial of white privilege, avoidance and/or hostility toward Nonwhites

The second community of origin in the continuum of responses to white supremacy within this model is that of the White Interracialist. This particular group in the sociotext representation can be described as having multiple relationships with the Nonwhite community either in the work place, the marketplace and/or the neighborhood. Their denial issue has its focus on the guilt and shame of their response to the white supremacy culture. Guilt arises when they realize that all persons in a society have a pervasive moral responsibility for the American family's racial dysfunction. The response of the White Interracial community is denial of any participation, approval of horrible crimes, or involvement in unjust social arrangements that disenfranchise Nonwhites. To make denial plausible the White population must deny it is enjoying social privileges that are based on the continuing oppression of Nonwhite people.[4] However, through encounters with Nonwhite people this population comes to realize that their access to the privileges of social, economic and political enfranchisement is dependent on their whiteness and their distance from the conditions of Nonwhites as a community.

Joseph Barndt gave an insight into his personal journey in the White liberal, interracial community;

At one time, because of a we/they mentality, I thought it was possible to separate white Americans into two camps: the righteous and the racist. I, of course, was a member of the righteous camp. I assumed that the occupants of each camp were there by choice. I believed that my friends and I had wisely chosen to be nonracists and those in the other camp had unwisely chosen to be racists. Now I know differently. I know there is no such thing as a nonracist camp. I know that, along with every other white

American, I am a racist and a member of the racist camp. I also know that most of us are not in this camp by choice. In many ways, we are prisoners in our own communities, prisoners of racism.[5]

The "camp" is our different communities of origin. Avoidance of the Nonwhite camp allows the distance to de-sensitize White awareness of the reality of Nonwhites. The resulting separation of the camps enhances the blindness and ignorance about the realities of how Nonwhites are pushed to the margins of society and allows a social innocence in the White camp. Self intervention on the denial mechanism allows the White Interracialist community to begin the journey from hurtful racial dysfunction to healing recovery. This journey is filled with resistance in our white supremacy culture. But we cannot begin our journey until we confront and challenge our denial.

The sociotext is a graphical representation of the various communities' response to the white supremacy culture (page 200). This representation of millions of behavorial daily response is a gross oversimplification of the reality as any graphic would be of a complex subject. However, it serves the purpose of highlighting that different communities have different responses within the same society. The sociotext is useful in seeing the different responses and range of responses within each community of origin. All of these responses cannot be catalogued here. An example of the range of responses can be seen in the example of one person's journey in the White community of origin. E.P. Ellis, a former Ku Klux Klan member, is a witness to the various positions that are lived out in a community. He talks about the support of the more educated members of his White community who encouraged the poorer, less educated White population in the Ku Klux Klan to do their bidding by attacking Nonwhite social advancement.

The majority of 'em are low-income whites, people who don't really have a part in something. They have been shut out as well as the blacks. Some are not very well-educated either. Just like myself. We had a lot of support from doctors and lawyers and police officers.[6]

The breadth of Ellis' experience in the White community is a journey from White Supremacist community to White Interracialist community and beyond to a community that has been referred to by some Whites as "race traitors." His experience represents the two main currents in the White community that are featured in the sociotext. However, there will be examples of people who go beyond the two main currents mentioned. The most important point to keep in mind is that there is a continuum of responses within each community from hostile to hospitable, from ferocious to friendly, and from enemies to engaged friends. The same can be said of the Nonwhite communities.

Nonwhite Responses to Denial

Nonwhite Interracialist Denial:
Denial of the effect of racism in my life

The Nonwhite interracialist group represented in the sociotext has various interactive relationships with Whites as neighbors, co-workers in the job force and in the marketplace. As shocking as the history and the present social inequalities of the white supremacy culture are against Nonwhites, denial is a mechanism also used by the communities who are victimized by racism. Nonwhites can be overwhelmed with the realization of what White agents, acting on behalf of white supremacy culture, can do to their lives, have done to their communities, and will do to maintain the status quo. Historically, most Whites would never be involved in brutal attacks or gross atrocities personally. Hate groups, social institutions and paramilitary forces are present to perform these deeds on their behalves.

The most common form of denial in the Nonwhite interracial community is the refusal to acknowledge the effects of racism in their lives. There are examples in the voices from the Black community that will point to certain successes and make a statement about their experience as being free of racism. Likewise, in the Hispanic/Latino community there are some voices declaring that racism is not the problem but discrimination. This denial comes from a fear of being considered anything other than White. In both examples from the Nonwhite community there is a denial of the reality of the various racisms touching their lives and the refusal to accept that they, too, are victims. Denial assists many in maintaining the concept of individual autonomy in a hostile environment while pursuing the goals of their lives. This denial allows Nonwhites to function on a day-to-day basis in collusion with the general American dysfunction in denial of the activities of the white supremacy culture. However, white denial is easier to maintain because of the seamless arrangement of social institutions that block the viewing of the oppression of Nonwhite populations.

An example of denial in the Nonwhite interracialist community can be seen in an incident involving Dr. Cornel West, a best-selling author on books relating to racism. This passage is taken from the preface of his book *Race Matters*.

I dropped my wife off for an appointment on 60th Street between Lexington and Park Avenues. I left my car, a rather elegant one in a safe parking lot and stood on the corner of 60th Street and Park Avenue to catch a taxi. I felt quite relaxed since I had an hour until my next engagement. At 5:00 P.M. I had to meet a photographer who would take the picture for the cover of this book on the roof of an apartment building in East Harlem on 115th Street and 1st Avenue. I waited and waited and waited. After the ninth taxi refused me, my blood began to boil. The tenth taxi refused me and stopped for a kind, well-dressed, smiling female fellow citizen of European descent. As she stepped in the cab, she said, "This is really ridiculous, is it not?" [7]

In this everyday event in New York City the denial from the perspective of the Nonwhite community lies in the assumption that the goods and services of society are available to everyone. The denial stage in this incident points out the "racisms" involved in a white supremacy culture. The primary story affecting the writer waiting for the cab is the story of the white supremacy response of the cab driver denying the humanity of the Nonwhite person. The secondary story is the response of the writer himself in assuming that he could, like Whites, find a cab as a Nonwhite person. It took several experiences of being passed by for him to accept the reality of racism in his face before he began to "boil" at the realization of his plight. A third form of denial is seen in the "female citizen of European descent." She takes advantage of his plight in the "go along to get along" form of social collusion.

Yet she is in denial of her white privilege by criticizing the cab driver's behavior as "ridiculous."

In this snapshot of the American family we see various "racisms" represented by three communities (perhaps, four if the cab driver is a recent immigrant) coming together and responding to the shared culture of white supremacy in their expressions of denial. Just as society shares the American racial dysfunction, recovery from racisms requires a family treatment that challenges the culture. Whether a cab driver, rider or someone left on the curb, we all are forced to address our American family dysfunction.

Nonwhite Supremacist Denial:
Denial that Whites are people both good and bad

In the Nonwhite supremacist community of origin, traditionally, the humanity of White people is denied. This action is a reaction to the surrounding white supremacy culture. It is a defense against being denied respect, denied life itself or the fullness of its possibilities. Denial in the Nonwhite supremacist community is not motivated by maintaining privilege as in the White community but for protection against the White community. Unlike the Nonwhite interracialist community it is not a denial motivated by the hope of succeeding in a White world. The denial of Whites as full human beings, brothers and sisters in the human family, is motivated by anger against the White community and is fueled by continuous frustration found within the white supremacy culture.

Colorist Response to
Denial of White Supremacy

The Colorist community is an emerging element in the discussion of race relations and racial dysfunction. Seldom has this community been discussed but its influence is felt wherever there is racial supremacy. The Colorist community refers to those who are born into the Nonwhite community but choose to "pass as White people" in the general population. Their option of passing is valued in the Nonwhite community and viewed as a threat to white privilege in the White community.

The term "Colorist" is taken from the book *The Color Complex:*

The Politics of Skin Color Among African Americans, a ground breaking work on the racial caste dynamics in the Nonwhite community. The Colorists are able to choose to embrace a white identity due to the lightness of their complexion, their white facial features and/or hair texture. Historically, the tradition of "passing" emerged in the American Indian and African communities where racial mixing produced offspring that possessed white physical traits. The offspring of racial mixing have been noted throughout the history of the United States. The offspring of an American Indian and a White were referred to as "half-breeds." In the African American community, the label for such offspring was "mulatto," borrowed from the Spanish; "Creole," borrowed from the French; and "high yellow," a term from the American South. Despite the number of people who chose to "pass as White," it was not the majority of those who could have done so.

Because of the laws of separation of the races a significant number of Nonwhites made their choice to advance their opportunities in the act of "passing as White." Gail Parrish, an African American writer from Detroit, Michigan, noted that her grandfather "passed" to advance the fortunes of his family. During the day he worked in downtown Chicago passing as a White man then returned to the Black community at night. She noted the widespread trend as it affected the country:

Census records show that from 1890 to 1910 there was a loss of 600,000 African Americans, or about 30,000 per year during that 20 year period. This disappearance of Blacks from the population has been attributed primarily to passing. It would be conservative to estimate that thousands of people continued to pass each year throughout the Jim Crow period.[8]

The Jim Crow period lasted almost 100 years, until the 1960s when new civil rights legislation began to overturn the tradition of racial separation by law. Certainly not all people having these traits sought or still seek to "pass." Therefore, the Colorists are only those who seek to "pass as White." Those members of the Nonwhite community who possess the looks to "pass as White" suffer from the racial dysfunction in unique ways. Historically, the lighter-skinned Native Americans, African Americans and

Hispanic Americans have played an intermediate role in the hemisphere between White people and the Nonwhite community. This intermediate role has varied from time to time. Sometimes the lighter-skinned have been trusted confidants of Whites and sell-outs to their respective communities of color. At other times, Nonwhites with physical traits that would allow them to pass have chosen to be leaders in the struggles of Nonwhites against Whites. And yet at the same time, the lighter-skinned members of the Nonwhite community are mistrusted by both the White community and the Nonwhite community in regards to which race do they have a true allegiance.

There is evidence that those Nonwhites who seek to "pass" were and are fulfilling a deep desire in the Nonwhite communities of origin. With the conquering of the Spanish in South America, there emerged a racial caste system that exalted white skin over brown or black skin. Dr. Samuel Betances, a Puerto Rican scholar, noted that one's white features can become one's ticket to success or failure.

Upward mobility was possible through racial mixing provided that in each interracial/ intercultural relationship the offspring continued to become more European Caucasian looking. The concept of "bettering the race" (mejorando la raza) has been an honored value in Hispanic/Latino society. If a black Negroid person married a Caucasian looking one, again the same principle applied. A mulatto (half-caste) or trigeno (color of wheat person) could improve their chances by also marrying into the ideal Caucasian group. Each level of "whitening" was recognized in the society by its particular blends. At times there were up to seventeen different categories.[9]

The influences of colorism are found throughout the hemisphere. In the view of some global commentators, there is an assumption that the United States has a great race problem and that the situation is better for Nonwhites in other countries in this hemisphere. In reality it is in the countries of Latin America and the Caribbean to the south where racial caste hierarchies are so immovable that many of their societies do not even possess civil rights for racial groups or voices to raise up a social justice movement. The Latin American claim of racial harmony is an empty boast offered to those who have never visited these places.

In North and South America the Colorist influence is a powerful current within the Nonwhite community and the source of many conflicts. Due to these conflicts there is a need to describe the Colorist response in the white supremacy culture and to identify those in the Nonwhite community who seek to implement a racial caste structure within the Nonwhite communities. This racial caste system within the Nonwhite communities of North and South America gives more value and respect to members in their community who possess the lighter and whiter shades of skin. The reality of this racial caste hierarchy within the Nonwhite communities can also be found in the Asian community,[10] the Black community in United States, the African diaspora[11] and the Hispanic/Latino community.[12]

Dr. Edwin J. Nichols, an expert on the psychology of Nonwhite and White dynamics, lectures in the area of racial caste psychology throughout the global village. A writer for a magazine captured the impact of Nichols' insight upon a Black federal employee who attended one of his presentations.

Matthew related a story he heard at an Edwin Nichols lecture about how messages of marrying someone lighter than ourselves were taught to many black children. These distinctions create differences between us and those we are close to — other black folk. Matthew's point is illustrated by current images of black males and females in rap videos. The men are brown-skinned and women have very light skin and have long hair. In this visual metaphor we see and hear the struggle with the self in a land where finding a light-skinned colored mate is the goal.[13]

The Colorist community within the Nonwhite community represents another unique response in white supremacy culture. Colorists are those who have nonwhite ancestry in their history but can "pass as White" in society due to the skin color, facial features and hair texture. The Colorists are those who use these physical features to gain access to social advantage and economic mobility. However, many people from the Asian, Black, Hispanic/Latino and Native American communities with these same features are not classified as Colorists. By definition a Colorist is one who is seeking to pass as White. Therefore, simply having the ability to be seen as White does not make a person a Colorist.

The advantage of White features in a white supremacy culture is a value not only in the White society but also in the Nonwhite society. Some Nonwhites seek after those in their community who have White features. They see a value in proximity to people who are White or lighter than themselves. This message is understood by lighter members of Nonwhite communities that their physical features are better than their peers in their respective Nonwhite community. The selection of lighter skinned women in Black music videos, which Matthew made reference to in his comment, represents an aspect of the Colorist dynamic within the Nonwhite community. It does not mean that the individuals in the video seek to be White but that the desire to have these particular skin types present by those with darker skin types demonstrates that light skin is a value by even those who do not possess it. [14] This is a common theme in the everyday racisms of the Nonwhite community.[15]

It is commonly thought that People of Color seek to "pass" as White. A growing collection of literature demonstrates that the Colorist community could form the largest minority group in the United States because the span of its membership includes those who are Nonwhites and seek whiteness through various strategies and those Nonwhites who, due to their complexion, are living with white status. In Jacobson's book *Whiteness of a Different Color: European Immigrants and the Alchemy of Race,* he presents a passage from Philip Roth's *Counterlife* in which a woman rejects the shows of affection by a Jewish man because she believes he is a Nonwhite.

"It is a racial matter," she insisted.

"No, we're the same race. You're thinking of Eskimos."

"We are not the same race. Not according to anthropologists, or whoever measures these things. There's Caucasian, Semitic-there are about five different groups. Don't look at me like that."

"But I am Caucasian, kiddo. In the U.S. census I am, for good or bad, counted as Caucasian."

"Are you? Am I wrong?" [16]

This exchange highlights the denial stage in the Colorist community and denial in the White Interracialist community. The Colorist denies their nonwhiteness to gain access to the benefits of society that comes in the form of social acceptance followed by success in one's life pursuits. At the same time, this conversation shows the ongoing struggle of those who have white status. Their privilege is realized in the fiction of a white identity that is tied to their collusion in the fiction of the nonwhite identity. Without the weight of the nonwhite identity upon which whiteness depends there would be no value in it. Maintaining white privilege commits the members of the society to do their part in denying the full humanity in the human family to those who do not possess white status.

Jacobson stresses in his work the arbitrary nature of the racial fictions of particular racial groups. He acknowledges that though race is a fiction, racism is a fact. To prop up this fiction the members of the society must collude constantly with the white supremacy culture by observing certain taboos that regulate their privileges in dating and other social interactions. He notes the lack of logic in the most accepted understanding around the fiction of race; that is, a White woman can have a Black child but a Black woman could never have a White child.

The Colorist attempts to use their whiteness as a privileged asset in a culture of white supremacy. There are untold millions in this group. The Colorist influence in our society, as they daily seek to pass as White and remain undetected by White and Nonwhites, is yet to be fully appreciated as a powerful current of our racial dysfunction.

The Intermediates Response
to White Supremacy Culture

The Intermediate community, as referred to in the Recovery from Racisms™ model, is the recent immigrant, the New American. This Intermediate community is an ally to the Colorist community and forms a continuum in the Colorist community from the perspective of a historical drive to white status to the new drive for white status. Just as Nonwhites have sought to "pass" as Whites by virtue of their skin color, so people who have immigrated to the United States from Europe have had to seek to be white also. Throughout the history of the United States, European immigrants were not always given white status upon arrival. Many of the immigrating groups have had to "pass" as Whites because the Anglo-Saxon Protestants did not see them as the right type of Whites. They were regarded as something other than "Whites", i.e., "White trash," "poor White," or in various ethnic terms. This period of time spent waiting to be accepted as White I have termed "intermediate." The idea is that the group is in a social limbo due to their immigrant arrival into a racial caste society that has not found a place for them. The dynamics of immigration to the United States today is playing out the same dynamic with several groups which find themselves in an intermediate status.

The work of the Intermediate group is to make itself acceptable to the "powers that be" or the "in-group" by their response to the white supremacy culture. Because the efforts of the Intermediate immigrants have a close parallel to the efforts of the Colorists, the responses of the two groups to the white supremacy culture have been placed together in the sociotext.

David Roediger chronicled in *The Wages of Whiteness: Race and the Making of the American Working Class* the efforts of the "intermediate status" which White immigrant groups have been forced to make to align themselves with the White "in-groups" to avoid being regarded and treated as the Nonwhite "out-group." Noel Ignatiev treated the same subject matter in *How the Irish Became White* and noted that when White immigrants to the United States saw that Blacks were at the bottom of the social ladder their response to white supremacy was to identify with whiteness and to distance themselves from Blacks socially and politically. The "intermediate" status of the Irish as a distinct ethnic group other than white kept them at a distance from the white establishment. This distance allows Whites to make them objects of derision like the "out group" experience of Blacks.

European immigrants were held in an "intermediate" status for many years. These groups included the Germans, the Irish, the Italians, the Poles, the Jews and many others. They were not initially considered White but eventually white status was conferred upon them. The process of conferral of whiteness is a mystery since legally there is no definition in the United States for what makes a person white. Given the intermediate status and the desire to be given white privilege, each community's response to white supremacy has its own dynamics and particular dysfunction of racism. The racial dysfunction in the Intermediate community was the imitation of the white community and fear of rejection while distancing themselves from other Nonwhites and fearing to associate with them. The intermediate community is conscious that it is not desirable for the dominant society to associate their group with a Nonwhite group because their social status is at risk. This particular dysfunction reinforces oppression for Nonwhite and assurance for Whites of their socially desirable privileges because the Intermediates internalize the beliefs of the white supremacy culture and stake their future upon it.

The social dynamics of the European immigrants' experience in the United States is the subject of new research in the area of Critical White Studies. Two examples of this exploration are by Theodore Allen and Karen Brodin. Allen's two-volume work *The Invention of the White Race* details the history of the origin of the Anglo-American system of race making in the early days of the republic onward. Brodin in her book *How the Jews Became White Folks and What That Says about Race in America* chronicles the social passage of Jews from being identified as a distinct ethnic group in the United States Census to disappearance by means of their acceptance into the whiteness of American suburban life. Jews became suburbanites and dropped from the United States Census as an Intermediate group. Blacks were kept out of this historic evolution of suburban culture in post-World War II America. The racial caste of the urban north became represented by the social icon of Black urban metropolises surrounded by White suburbs. The reality of the "colorline" that W. E. DuBois, the famous Black intellectual, predicted at the beginning of the 20th century was once again brought to bear after the Second World War. The racial caste system in United States society and racial polarization in the largest urban centers of the civilization was reinforced through social reorganization for the succeeding half century. This area of Critical White Studies is developing an American family tree of the racial caste system in its origin and its contemporary manifestation.

As will all communities, the Intermediate and Colorist groups need to recover from their internalization of the racial hierarchy of the culture. These two groups are seldom identified in discussions of racism which are usually framed as Black and White issues. When the term Intermediate is used alone it will refer to those immigrant groups who have not had white status conferred on them.[17]

Colorist Denial: Denial of their nonwhiteness

The twentieth century opened with literature citing the favorable reaction to light-skinned Blacks as being more likely to succeed due to their White blood. This attitude and the consequences of this response to white supremacy in both the White and Nonwhite communities of origin have created a Colorist community. The history and social dynamics of the Colorist is the focus of the book *The Color Complex: The Politics of Skin Color Among African Americans* by Kathy Russell, Midge Wilson and Ronald Hall. This contemporary ground breaking work gave an informed and highly needed understanding of a hidden American nation/family dysfunction that is part of our collective family psychological history. According to the writers:

Several interrelated factors explain the "light at the top" phenomena in Black American leadership. In a society that is politically and economically controlled by Whites, those members of minorities with the lightest skin and the most Caucasian-looking features have been allowed the greatest freedom. The unique privileges granted to mulattoes under slavery enabled them to advance further, educationally and occupationally, than Blacks who were dark skinned. The result was a leadership pool of light-skinned Blacks with both money and education. Within that pool, it was often those Blacks light enough to pass (as White) who became the Black community's most vocal and active leaders.[18]

In-group and out-group designates the point at which a person will be located within the circle of equity in a system. When European and other immigrants to the United States saw that Blacks were at the bottom of the racial caste hierarchy, they chose to aspire to be part of the White in-group and to keep a social distance between themselves and Blacks. Their "intermediate" status was between being considered White and being in the out-group as Blacks were and are considered.

The Intermediates need to recover from their adoption of the color caste hierarchy of white supremacy. The intermediate status of "almost but not quite" is seen in terms of names given to recent immigrants such as "sand niggers" for Arabs, "dirty wetbacks" for Hispanics/Latinos. The issue of colorism for nonwhite denial is complicated by the threat of oppression if one's "out-group" status is admitted. An example can be seen in the treatment of the native populations in Central and South American countries and in Mexico with its Chiapas revolution. The attempt to deny nonwhiteness can mean more than social and economic advancement. It can mean the difference between life and death. In an interview with Chief Billy Redwing Tayac, the pressure on the Native Americans to deny their nonwhiteness is described as being beyond the daily experience of racism for most Whites and Nonwhites in North America.

Governments don't like to classify these people as Indians. What some call mestizos, Hispanics or Chicanos are really Indians. They are not classified that way because of paper genocide. They would prefer to kill them, as with the 38,000 killed in the 1930's in El Salvador. Everyone who looked a certain way or who wore certain clothing was shot and killed indiscriminately. Mexicans today with dark complexions and black hair will deny they are Indians. They will say, "I am a Mexican." They have been brainwashed, because the lowest people on the ladder are the Indians. Who wants to be part of that group? [19]

This understanding of the Hispanic/Latino experience can give insight to the denial of Native American heritage and identification with the Nonwhite community. This response to white supremacy has marked their reality in such a traumatic and sustained manner that denial is a tool of personal survival and can be a communal attempt to avoid forms of genocide.

In the literature the assumption of a white identity by a Non-white person is termed as "passing," as in "passing for White." It has been noted that many groups who are considered Nonwhites attempt to "pass."[20] Stanley Lieberson noted the phenomenon of "passing" among European immigrants who were not Anglo-Saxons. These immigrants were "intermediates," in other words they were ethnics in a racial hierarchy that were not yet considered White. To deny their nonwhiteness and to access the privileges of the White "in-group," they strategized a way of "passing."

There are a variety of interaction situations in which European ethnic origin is less clearly marked, whereas in all face-to-face situations the vast majority of blacks are marked. The exception, for the latter, are of course those who "pass." But the interesting feature here is that the new groups may unintentionally pass in a variety of situations without making any effort to do so, such as changing their surnames; namely, there are many public instances where determination of ethnic origin among whites is impossible.[21]

Lieberson goes on to list many ethnic figures who changed their names to more Anglo-Saxon ones to "pass" as "All American." Some of them are listed below.

Stage Name	Original Name
Jerry Lewis	Joseph Levitch
Doris Day	Doris Kapplehoff
Tony Curtis	Bernie Schwartz
Judy Garland	Frances Gumm
Ginger Rogers	Virginia McMath
Ethel Merman	Ethel Zimmerman
Vic Damone	Vito Farinola
Rita Hayworth	Margarita Carmen Cansino
Donna Reed	Donna Mullenger
June Allyson	Ella Geisman
Kirk Douglas	Issur Danielovitch
Danny Kay	Daniel Kaminsky
Dean Martin	Dino Crocetti

The recovery issue for the Intermediate is to realize their distaste for their status as Nonwhites and accept the value of their humanity over the fictions of race and the strategies of collusion.

Conclusion on Denial

Denial is the first obstacle in the intervention treatment for racial dysfunction. Intervening in racial dysfunction involves gaining new insight into understanding one's personal denial issues. Through this personal insight we can begin to accept our responsibility to collaborate in the reconstruction of our culture in such a way as to reunite the human family. This New Family Formation process demands that we recognize the full humanity of all people which racisms deny.

Intervening in denial on both the personal level and the cultural levels is the most important and difficult task of recovery from racisms. This denial is formed within the culture of the various communities of origin and acted out by individuals of these different racial, ethnic and cultural backgrounds. Each racial, ethnic and cultural group has a history of adapting and coping with the white supremacy culture in which we live: White, Nonwhite, Intermediate/Colorist. Therefore, an understanding on the intervention issues for the racialized self from one community would be very difficult to comprehend by a person from another community. To this observation of guessing the mind of a person from a different community of origin add the further complication of understanding persons from within the same racial community of origin. Within the White community there are differences in beliefs about the role of white supremacy in their lives. And in the Nonwhite community there is the dynamic of "internalized oppression." This term describes those Nonwhites who have adopted the behavior of the white supremacy culture towards members of their own community.

Recovery from Racisms™ is a personal work that can benefit social transformation. Caution is necessary. Many people in an effort to do social transformation focus on changing others but not themselves. Like any form of recovery we can look at the splinter in other's eyes and overlook the log in our own. Therefore it would be difficult to examine another person's behavior to know his/her stage of recovery from racisms. The sociotext is presented to demonstrate that everyone in the society has racial dysfunction issues to address. The place to start to address those issues is within one's self. There is enough work there for a lifetime of recovery. This does not take away the value of the overview of a description of the behaviors that can be observed from the various communities of origin. It does help to locate ourselves in the larger picture of our society and communities to begin the personal transformation that leads to social transformation. The caution in the use of the sociotext is made to call attention to where the transformation begins in this particular model of antiracism work. It begins with personal transformation and moves to social transformation.

The first area of resistance in the recovery from racisms is denial. It is important to understand that denial challenges any discovery of the other four stages in the intervention process: anger, bargaining, depression and acceptance. The denial mechanism guards these stages and provides energy to resist the exploration of them. Just as in any family working through its dysfunctions, denial becomes a tool to resist moving from hurts to healing. From whatever perspective that denial is understood, be that personal, cultural or global, it delays the recovery process which is surely needed in our country and the world.

The following chapters will journey through the stages of recovery as seen in five communities of origin: White Supremacist, White Interracialist, Nonwhite Interracialist, Nonwhite Supremacist and Intermediate/Colorist. Throughout the stages of intervention there will be an element of denial. Each stage beyond denial provides more light along the path of racial dysfunction as we journey to racial sobriety.

1   Ridgeway, J.(1990). *Blood in the Face: The Ku Klux Klan, Aryan Nations, Nazi Skinheads, and the Rise of a New White Culture.* (New York: Thunder's Mouth Press. 13-16.

2   Ibid.

3   Ridgeway, 81.

4   McIntosh, P. (1993). White Privilege: Unpacking the Invisible Knapsack (In Peace and Freedom. July/August, 1989 pp. 10-13). Dismantling Racism: Work Book For Social Change Group. A. Ayvazian, K. Jones and E. Rankin. Amherst, Massachusetts, The Exchange Project Peace Development Fund.

5   Barndt, J. (1991). *Dismantling Racism: The Continuing Challenge to White America.* Minneapolis: Augsburg Fortress Publisher. 43.

6   Terkel, S. (1992). *Race: How Blacks and Whites Think and Feel about the American Obsession.* New York: The New Press. 272.

7   West, C. (1993). *Race Matters.* Boston, MA, Beacon Press. Preface x.

8   See the Michigan Chronicle Newspaper, "'Passing': Whose Shame?" March 27. A-4.

9   Betances, S. (1997). "African-Americans and Hispanics/Latinos: Eliminating Barriers to Coalition Building." People of the Pyramids: The Dialogue Between the African American and the Hispanic/Latino Communities. 27.

10 Lee,J. (1997) *Performing Asian America: Race and Ethnicity on the Contemporary Stage.* Philadelphia: Temple University Press.

11 Fanon, F. (1963). *The Wretched of the Earth.* New York: Grove Press, Inc.,Fanon, F. (1967). *Black Skin, White Mask.* New York: Grove Press.; Russell, K., M. Wilson, et al. (1992). *The Color Complex: The Politics of Skin Color Among African Americans.* New York: Harcourt Brace Jovanovich.

12 Rodriguez, R. (1982). *Hunger of Memory: The Education of Richard Rodriguez, An Autobiography.* New York: Bantam Windstone.; Rodriquez, R. (1991). "La Raza Cosmica." New Perspectives Quarterly Winter: 47-51.; Abalos, D. T. (1986). *Latinos in the United States: The Sacred and the Political.* Notre Dame, IN: University of Notre Dame Press.

13 Jones, S. E. (1994). Black Men: Connections & Disconnections. The Public Manager-The New Bureaucrat. 24.

14 Russell, K., M. Wilson, et al. (1992). *The Color Complex: The Politics of Skin Color Among African Americans.* New York: Harcourt Brace Jovanovich.

15 Delgado, R., Ed. (1995). *Critical Race Theory: The Cutting Edge.* Philidelphia: Temple University Press.

16 Jacobson, M. (1998). *Whiteness of a Different Color: European Immigrants and the Alchemy of Race.* Cambridge, MA: Harvard University Press.

17 Hacker, A. (1992). *Two Nations.* New York: Scribners.

18 Russell, K., M. Wilson, et al. (1992). *The Color Complex: The Politics of Skin Color Among African Americans.* New York: Harcourt Brace Jovanovich. 34-35.

19 Bigelow, B., Ed. (1992). *Interview with Chief Tayac: Struggles Unite Native Peoples. Rethinking Columbus: Teaching About the 500th Anniversary of Columbus Arrival in America.* Milwaukee, WI, Rethinking Schools. 57)

20 Harris, C. L. (1993). "Whiteness as Property." The Harvard Law Review.; Featherstone, E., Ed. (1994). *Skin Deep: Women Writing on Color, Culture, and Identity.* Freedom California, The Crossing Press.; Delgado, R., Ed. (1995). Critical Race Theory: The Cutting Edge. Philadelphia, Temple University Press.

21 Lieberson, S. (1980). *A Piece of The Pie: Blacks and White Immigrants Since 1880.* Berkley, CA, University of California Press.

Anger

Anger
   When a desired goal is frustrated, the emotional response is anger. Racial anger is seen most often when a person's self-esteem is at stake.

Voices of Anger

   When I recall my racial awakening, it is with a lot of anger. I was raised in mixed neighborhoods until entering high school. I attended a high school that was 99% Black. I did not have a problem with that as a Black female myself. However, when I shared with others that I had White friends and neighbors, the people around me began to mock me. I realized that the things they were saying were negative and full of hostility. They said there was something wrong with me if I played with White kids. They called me names like "Uncle Tom" and "Whitey lover." I came home crying. I did not understand what the problem was (the idea of interracial hostility). My mom convinced me that everything was going to be OK, and that I would meet other people who would be my friends. I was brought up in mixed neighborhoods and schools, at that time I did not know there was supposed to be a difference that drew a line between Black and White people. I experience anger every time I recall this racial awakening.

– Black female

~ • ~

I was rapidly walking through the halls of the main office with several work issues on my mind and an appointment with a supervisor within the next several minutes. A co-worker stopped me in mid stride and stated that in her culture it was polite to acknowledge other people when you walk by them. I explained that I had a great deal on my mind and was not intentionally ignoring her. She then stated that she would appreciate it if I did not do this again. Soon after this, I became intensely angry with this person not so much because of any blatant rudeness but because I felt that she wanted me to acknowledge her culture when she apparently had no consideration for my culture (upbringing may be more accurate than culture) or the fact that I had a great deal on my mind. Unfortunately for the next several months I made it a point to acknowledge everyone around this person without acknowledging her.

This is an example of how I became angry when confronted about my apparent rudeness to another culture's rules of politeness. Although there may have been other things happening in my head, given the experience this person had of white supremacy, my attitude was coming across as if I were discounting her value and arrogant.

– White male

~ • ~

I still experience the anger I felt when I remember what happened during our honeymoon in Washington DC. My husband and I went to a restaurant, the waitress who was serving us, purposefully spilled a glass of water on us. The waitress who was an

African American did not apologize but looked at us with a lot of resentment. I guess she resented my husband who is an African-American with a light complexion, being with anyone other than an African American woman. I am from Central America with a Chinese father.

– Hispanic/Asian female

~ • ~

I become outraged, sad, and angry whenever I reflect and ponder on one of the saddest chapters in my family's history in which both of my maternal grandparents were taken away from their families while they were young children and forced to live at government residential boarding schools until they finished high school. Their rationale was that it would be better for Native American children (and for United States society as a whole) if their Native identity and cultures were eradicated and they were integrated into the mainstream American melting pot.

My grandparents suffered great personal pain and trauma because of being forcibly separated from their families and homes. They were victims of emotional and physical (and possibly sexual) abuse. The cruel treatment that they endured had a catastrophic effect on them and on their children and on subsequent generations which continues to reverberate throughout my family to this day.

– Native American male

Personal Examination

Unaware

Do I become anxious or angry when faced with a racial situation?

Aware

Am I willing to admit that certain racial situations can cause a great emotional reaction in me?

Self Aware

My racial anger arises to call my attention to what issues in my life?

The Anger Stage

When a desired goal is frustrated the emotional response is anger. This is the second stage of intervention in recovery from racisms. Anger is seen most often when a person's self interest is at stake, especially in social and economic issues. Anger results when denial can no longer be used to keep an issue at a distance. Dr. Kubler-Ross describes the progression from denial to anger in her original model.

When the first stage of denial cannot be maintained any longer, it is replaced by feelings of anger, rage, envy, and resentment. The logical next question becomes: "Why me?" [1]

The "Why me?" response captures at the personal level an attack on one's self esteem. Racial anger arises on a social level when people experience a loss of their sense of the status quo due to racial issues. Whether the personal attack or social loss is real or imagined, a sense of privilege or respect has been violated. From the recovery from racisms viewpoint, anger is a response to a loss in one or more of the following areas:

• loss of self-importance, for example, due to a change in the status quo of racial interaction

• loss of self-perfection, for example, perceived as being a bigot, being racially profiled for screening, etc.

• loss of power, imagined or real, due to race, for example, voting irregularities, neighborhood change, etc.

• loss of social independence due to issues such as fear of crime, police harassment, segregation or integration, etc.

A feeling of loss in any of these areas can become a "river of anger" for a person or a community.[2] The situations that trigger the perception of loss vary from one community of origin to another. But the emotional reaction is the same, that of anger. In this section a survey of the various faces of racial anger is presented.

White Response to Anger in White Supremacy Culture

White Supremacist Anger:
Anger that Nonwhites enjoy some degree of enfranchisement

The face of anger can be seen in the White supremacist community when white privileges are seen as under threat of loss.[3] Anger is also triggered when white privileges are extended to Nonwhites. This anger is seen by some Whites as "righteous indignation" that someone other than a White person is enjoying white entitlements. In 1986 Evelyn Rich interviewed David Duke, the noted White supremacist from Louisiana, and uncovered this anger.

We don't want Negroes around. We don't need Negroes around... We simply want our own country and our own society. " He also said that the American economy is dominated by "...Jews, Jews, Jews, and more Jews. They raped the country economically....I don't have any hatred toward the average Jew. I think I've got a lot of enmity toward the Jews as a whole. I resent what they're doing. I resent them.[4]

These views still have an audience despite the political correctness of our times. Groups that promote hatred and bigotry are demanding rights to march through cities and exercise their right to preach hate. However, the extreme White supremacist represents only one point on a continuum of the White communities' issues of racial anger as a form of racial dysfunction.

White Interracialist Anger:
Anger when their racism (blatant or latent) is pointed out

The "White Interracialist" is a designation on a continuum of behavior that historically has had a wide range of responses. These responses include speaking out for tolerance, equality, and the dismantling of racism in our society. In this continuum of Whites, statements can range from the acceptance of Nonwhites as equal persons in society to the strong condemnation of white racism. An example of this condemnation is the magazine for the "New White Abolitionists," *Race Traitor,* for those who desire to leave the white race and join the human race. One of the movement's leaders is a Harvard professor, Noel Ignatiev.[5] From whatever community of origin one finds oneself there is a need for intervention on the stage of anger. Two race relation leaders, Joseph Barndt and Charles Ruehle comment in *America's Original Sin* on the White Interracialist's anger.

Robert Terry, antiracism trainer and author, states in Impacts of Racism on White Americans: "I am not personally offended when someone says being white in America makes me a white racist. That is true. I am offended, however, if someone says that is all that I am. That is not true. I am both a racist and an antiracist, and, as an antiracist, strongly committed to the elimination of racism".[6]

The anger that Terry describes here is an emotion that has been processed over years. Although Terry is a dedicated trainer in anti-racism the accusation nonetheless is an offense to him and his response of anger is due to a loss of self-esteem in light of his efforts in personal healing. Terry's comment also is a testimony to the ongoing need to deepen the journey of recovery. One's awareness is only the beginning of a long and continually revealing jouney.

The difference in the sociotext between anger in the White supremacist community and the White interracialist community is the cause from which the anger arises. The issue of anger in the White supremacist community is the perceived loss of white privilege in their world. On the other hand, in the White interracialist community the focus of anger is likely to be a form of attack on the person's self-image. In this case, the threatened loss is that of social innocence due to accusations of collusion with the white supremacy culture in their racial attitudes and behaviors. The everyday social location of white supremacy anger is usually at a distance from the Nonwhite population while the interracialist anger often occurs in the midst of face-to-face racial interactions.

Nonwhite Response to Anger in the White Supremacy Culture

Nonwhite Interracialist: Anger at the realization that racism has circumscribed and impacted their life from birth

Similar to the white interracialist anger at being viewed only by their white racial identity the anger of the Nonwhite interracialist mirrors of the same reality. The nonwhite interracialist anger arises out of the experience of being circumscribed, that is, being confined by a white supremacy culture in which their life choices are limited everyday. The limitations include employment advancement, educational entitlement, political enfranchisement and social prestige as social actors in theater of daily life. An example of this nonwhite interracialist anger can be witnessed in the book *Race Matters* by Cornell West.

Ugly racial memories of the past flashed through my mind. Years ago, while driving from New York to teach at Williams College, I was stopped on fake charges of trafficking cocaine. When I told the police officer I was a professor of religion, he replied "Yeh, and I'm the Flying Nun. Let's go, nigger!" I was stopped three times in my first ten days in Princeton for driving too slowly on a residential street with a speed limit of twenty-five miles per hour. (And my son, Clifton, already has similar memories at the tender age of fifteen.) [7]

Nonwhite interracialists are confronted by situations from which anger arises on every level of existence, from the interpersonal to the global. They are faced with losses of self-esteem and the various means that build it, such as power, independence and the pursuit of happiness.

Nonwhite Supremacist: Anger that Nonwhites
do not see what White society is perpetrating

The Nation of Islam since its origins decades ago until recently has been considered an example of the nonwhite supremacist expression. However, today the image is just one more representation on the continuum of beliefs by Whites and Nonwhites. The Nation of Islam's most well known spokesperson of yesterday was Malcolm X who was assassinated in 1965. Today, forty years after his death, his memory and work to uplift the Black/Nonwhite community are experiencing a rebirth in intellectual and popular culture. A member of the Nation reflects on sentiments that captured their anger issues of the 60's and 70's.

Often at the temple we would speak of the dead, but we weren't talking about black people who had in fact died and been buried in a cemetery, says Benjamin Karim, we were talking about the "the so-called American negroes" who lived in ignorance of themselves and their condition. We might also call them the deaf, dumb, and blind because the so-called American negroes failed to use their senses—or their sense—in dealing with the white society that was continually oppressing them.[8]

This example of Nonwhite supremacist anger is directed at the Nonwhite community's collusion with the white supremacy culture. It mirrors White supremacist anger against other White people who are seen as "race traitors." And in the same way, the secondary target of anger is the society at a distance, from both the Nonwhite and White supremacists. Unfortunately, as with many forms of anger, those closest to the angry people get the initial force of it. The anger of the Nonwhite supremacist seeks to be a call to action to the Nonwhite community rather than to challenge the "powers that be" directly.

A Global example of nonwhite supremacist anger can be seen in the work of Albert Memmi *The Colonizer and the Colonized*. Memmi analyzes the French colonization of North Africa and the Muslims living there in the revolution of the late 1950's. Though he was living in France at the time he identified himself with the colonized Muslims in the revolt. He describes the colonized as having a slave "mentality" and expresses the powerlessness of the nonwhite supremacist position. It is significant that Memmi dedicates the 1965 edition of his book to "the American Negro, also colonized,..." Generally, the cause of Nonwhite supremacist anger is the victimization of their respective community and the internalization of the white supremacy culture in the attitudes and actions of the Nonwhite community.

Colorist/Intermediate Response to Anger in White Supremacy Culture

Colorist/Intermediate: Anger when their humanity is denied or confined based on their nonwhiteness

The racial anger of the Colorist and Intermediate community is provoked when there is an attempt to discover their nonwhite identity or uncover their ethnic group. The anger can arise from either Whites or Nonwhites who choose to inquire, comment or confront the person or group about their racial or ethnic heritage.

The Intermediate/Colorist is a member of a community that is Nonwhite but is seeking to be viewed as White or "pass" as White in social interactions. Historically those who have been able to "pass" as White were those Native Americans and African Americans who possessed a light complexion and European facial features. However, European immigrants who were not considered White on their arrival to the United States could attempt to "pass" as White by changing their ethnic names to something that was "more American" or Anglo-Saxon.

Changing one's name and assuming the appearance of whiteness are only two of the most popular strategies for "passing" that are used today. For some Hispanics/Latinos it is guarding against the suntan that could give evidence of their Indian racial background as Richard Rodriguez shares in his autobiography. In a workshop on antiracism in the Hispanic/Latino community, different participants related how Hispanics/Latino youths who were English-speaking could "pass" when working in the suburbs as White. One method was combing one's hair in such a way as to take on the appearance of a "white ethnic," such as an Italian or Greek. This ability to "pass" was a bargaining chip for employment. In an environment of White supremacists, as one participant noted, the young suburban skinheads would pass you by if you did not look Hispanic/Latino.

Intermediate/Colorist anger is a response to a loss of self-esteem or other perceived loss. This is most often a response to a perceived loss of power associated with white status, and the loss of opportunities for success given by the power to pass as white. This experience includes new immigrant groups who would be considered "White" in appearance but have not yet been granted white status in terms of social acceptance and white privilege by both White and Nonwhite citizens.

Conclusion on Anger

Anger is a common response to frustration and loss, real or imagined. Anger is a natural response that attempts to restore power in the face of a challenge. Initially anger restores self-esteem and physical presence to a challenging situation. Anger as a stage in the Recovery from Racisms' perspective is viewed as the response to a loss of one's life possibilities due to one's racialized identity.

Racial anger has as many faces as the various communities of origin in a society. In the white supremacy culture in which we live racial anger has many triggers in any given situation. The triggers of racial anger in the various White communities of origin often center around the loss of white privilege and lost social innocence. The triggers for racial anger in the Nonwhite communities are often the loss of opportunity to advance towards enfranchisement due to their nonwhite status. Enfranchisement here means access to the avenues of society's resources that are open to all those with white status.[9]

The anger around race relations, and the lack thereof, give rise to tremendous energy that ravages our society in its aftermath. The racial anger of the American family's dysfunction unfolds as an alphabet of negative feelings and actions. An Alphabet of Racial Dysfunction would include the following letters and description of the horrendous actions and their consequences: A for Anger over everything from unfounded accusations to zenophobic hysteria; B for Blaming "the racial other" as the scapegoat for "the problems"; C for Calling names and castigating entire groups; D for Demonizing others as the evil in our midst; E for Elimination of the "other" from our lives and society; F for Forgetting about the other (lock them in jail and throw away the key); and the letters of this alphabet go on and on. Not only does the Alphabet of Racial Dysfunction generate more and more illness, the anger produced around other social dysfunctions such as sexism, classism and ageism also fill our lives with "stinking thinking" about our brothers and sisters. Just as we need racial sobriety so as not to "live under the influence" of anger, we need to extend it to every hurt of our society. Simply put, we need to live – S-O-B-E-R; that is, Seeing Others as Being Entitled to Respect. Anger as a restorative emotion is our inner cry for respect. Establishing a culture of racial sobriety can lead to a much needed cultural change where racial anger can be quieted because of our sober living in regards to race, gender, class and age. Racial sobriety as "seeing each person as my brother and sister" is the first step in an American family therapy aimed at a sober lifestyle of "Seeing Others as Being Entitled to Respect."

1   Kubler-Ross, E. (1973). *On Death and Dying.* New York: Macmillan Company. 44.

2   Rohrer, N. and S. P. Sutherland (1981). *Facing Anger.* Minneapolis, Augsburg Publishing House.

3   Ibid. Rohrer & Sutherland 1981.

4   Collum, D. D. (1992). Fascism With A Facelift: Racist Ideology in the Political Mainstream. America's Original Sin. B. Hulteen and J. Wallis. Washington, D. C. : Sojourners. 150-151.

5   (1994). Treason to Witness is Loyalty to Humanity: An Interview with Noel Ignatiev of Race TraitorM Magazine. Utne Reader

6   Barndt, J. and C. Ruehle (1992). Rediscovering a Heritage Loss : A European-American Anti-racist Identity. America's Original Sin. B. Hulteen and J. Wallis. Washington, D. C. : Sojourners. 76.

7   West, C. (1993). *Race Matters.* Boston, MA, Beacon Press. Preface ix.

8   Karim, B. P. Skutches, et. al. (1992.) *Remembering Malcolm.* New York: One World Ballentine Books. 80.

9   Ignatiev, N. (1995). *How the Irish Became White.* New York: Routledge; Lieberson, S. (1980). *A Piece of The Pie: Blacks and White Immigrants Since 1880.* Berkley, CA: University of California Press.

Bargaining

Bargaining is the act of "going along to get along" with the white supremacy culture in order to gain social acceptance, economic security and power in a society dominated by racial caste interactions.

Voices of Bargaining

While I was in Mexico this summer living with Mexican nationals in their Community I was constantly asked what it was like being Mexican-American. I realized that the reason they were asking me this question is because they could not situate me as one of them. I explained to them that I felt very marginalized as a Mexican-American because I was never fully accepted as a United States American because of my color and heritage and that when I was in Mexico, I was never fully accepted as Mexican because of my United States American way of being. I told them how I always found myself bargaining to fit in both cultures. I see now how this marks my "two-ness" in a world of white supremacy and in a culture of high nationalism.

Every time I bargain to fit in I have to deny a certain part of myself, in the way I speak or express myself. It is hard for people to grasp what it means to straddle two cultures; it is even more difficult for a transcultural individual to grasp what is happening to him/her when engaging within a dominant cultural mindset. Bargaining is always taking place when I realize that I am "other" and not quite "one of us." The way I have come to experience healing is by sharing my story. My recovery is in process because I have discovered power in being able to articulate my journey and I am no longer ashamed of telling people what being marginalized or discriminated against has cost me.

– Hispanic/Latino male

~•~

In developing the composition of a board I served on, the realization struck me that I was bargaining over the issue of how many Whites to put on the board in relation to people of color. It was obvious to me that bargaining was going on when I selected the respective roles that Whites and people of color would hold: Whites would have access to power and money, while people of color would give cover and credibility to the effort.

I chose this situation because it is most likely to be played out in many of my public relation efforts. I also realized that people participating would see this manipulation, and I would be challenged to resolve it through recruitment of more members to the board that could ensure a balance in trust and confidence in all the members.

– White male

~•~

When I attended the State University, which is a predominately white university, I was determined to make good grades. When I took a test, I would make sure that my score was high just in case one of my classmates who was White asked me my score. I was bargaining with the good White folks. "Look at me, I am an African American, and I am smart." I was bargaining to be seen as an exception. I was bargaining for acceptance.

– Black female

~•~

When spending time with my birth family and even more so with my in-laws (southern White) I find myself down playing my own recovery, and the work I do in anti-bias, prejudice reduction and Recovery from Racisms. I see this as bargaining, as I "go along to get along" to keep peace in the family and protect myself from negative challenges/attacks on my values from family members.

– White female

Personal Examination

Unaware

Do I find myself agreeing to people's racial comments when I really do not agree, just to keep the peace?

Aware

What situation comes to mind for me when I think about my racial bargaining?

Self Aware

How does my racial bargaining work for my personal gain?

The Bargaining Stage

Racial bargaining in the Recovery from Racisms™ stages deals with the life choices people make as they collude with white supremacy. To collude, in terms of racial dysfunction, means to "go along to get along" with the racial taboos and rules of the social order. The issue in the racial bargaining process is the question: How can I take advantage of the social and political arrangements in a white supremacy culture so as to enjoy its privileges? In other words: How can I access the avenues of power, economic entitlement and social esteem in my everyday life?

For the White supremacist the best way to society's benefits is seen as maintaining one's white status. This white status also insures that their offspring will inherit these privileges through a social strategy of separation from Nonwhites so as to protect the valuable asset of "pure blood." A common strategy of apartheid is social distance through segregation and a racial caste hierarchy. Segregation is a strategy that maintains separate spaces to limit the contact between Whites and Nonwhites. When social interaction cannot be avoided, there are specified roles for Whites and Nonwhites make up a racial caste hierarchy in which White actors dominate Nonwhite actors.

Racial bargaining involves all the communities of a society. As South Africa began to emerge from its apartheid, one of their most well known citizen, Nozipho Mfeka, an award winning model and writer, was interviewed on the comparison of racism in her country and the United States.

The beautiful thing about America is that there are only two races: White and Black. In South Africa there are four: White, Indian, Colored and Black, in the so-called order of superiority. So if you were black you experienced racism from three different angles! You were teased about your hair, full lips and flat nose... If you were black you received the worst treatment! ... And now with Affirmative Action and other actions in favor of the Black race, those two races: Indians and Colored cling closer to the Black side (Laughing). Just a group of confused people![1]

Just as other countries have white supremacy cultures, the United States also faces the consequences of groups racially bargaining their way through a maze of relationships. Though the United States does not have as many racial castes as India or the 14 levels of Coloreds in South Africa,[2] there is certainly an increasing diversity of racial and ethnic groups competing with one another.

White Response to Bargaining in White Supremacy Culture

White Supremacist Bargaining: Whiteness is protected by the separation and avoidance of Nonwhite people

The context for racial bargaining in the White supremacist community of origin is that of protecting the privilege accorded to white status. Despite the cost to self, to the family or to Nonwhites, the value of being white is to be upheld. An example of the bargaining process can be seen in the insights of E. P. Ellis, who was a member of the Ku Klux Klan, who rejected this association and now supports unity and dignity of the races. He recalls his initiation into the Klan in Durham, North Carolina.

I was led into a large meeting room and this was the time of my life! It was thrilling. Here's a guy who's worked hard all his life and struggled all his life to be something, and here's the moment to be something. I will never forget it. Four robed Klans men led me into the hall. The light(s) were dim and all you could see was an illuminated cross. I knelt before the cross. I had to make certain vows and promises. We promised to uphold the purity of the white race, fight communism, and protect white womanhood.[3]

The "purity of the white race" is the cornerstone of white bargaining in America. In the Spanish conquest of the Americas, the blood lines of individuals were noted in the records of baptism so that no one who was not pure white was eligible for public office or could enter the life of a Catholic priest, sister or brother. In an attempt to level the playing field, Hispanic/Latino culture developed the concept of "mejorando la raza," improving the race by marrying someone whose skin was lighter than their own. Through the whitening of the family's complexion and marriage into families with purer Spanish blood, social acceptance and enfranchisement could be gained.[4]

The underlying value of a white supremacy culture is the "purity of the white race." The White supremacist community bargains daily to construct societies to protect it. This idea of the "white race" is not fixed in color but on the false belief of color determining who is to be treated as a full human being. A lack of sobriety diminishes others, and those who perpetrate this action are living under the influence of "stinking thinking."

An example of white supremacy culture not being related to color, but to who is considered a human being, would be that of Benjamin Franklin. Franklin was a "Founding Father" of the nation and an outspoken and published White supremacist. Roger Daniels, in his history of immigration and ethnicity entitled, *Coming to America*, presents Franklin's appeal of 1751. It racialized and demonized the German immigrants entering Pennsylvania in colonial times.

...Why should Pennsylvania, founded by the English, become a Colony of Aliens, who will shortly be so numerous as to Germanize us instead of our Anglifying them, and will never adopt our language or Customs, nay more than they can acquire our Complexion.

...And in Europe, the Spaniards, Italians, French, Russians and Swedes, are generally of what we call a swarthy Complextion; as are Germans also, the Saxons only accepted, who with the English, make the principal Body of White People on the Face of the Earth. I could wish their numbers were increased.[5]

Franklin articulated the White supremacist community's core belief of separation from, and avoidance of Nonwhites, despite the white skin they possess. He lacked racial sobriety in regards to the German immigrants and other Europeans. He was not sober; that is, not able to See Others as Being Entirely Real as himself. His lack of racial sobriety had him thinking, feeling and acting under the influence of racial dysfunction. Clearly, white supremacy culture is not about the color of the person's skin. It is about who has their humanity denied and given a fictionalized identity, so as to be regarded as someone other than our brother or sister. Racial labels fictionalize and can demonize a people's true humanity. Once we have fictionalized or demonized a group through racial labels, the freedom to attack and destroy "the other" can occur without reason, restraint or regret. In fact, we can go about the destruction of others with a feeling of righteousness. Racial sobriety is a commitment to be sober – "Seeing Others as Being Entirely Real" to us.

White Interracialist Bargaining

White Interracialist Bargaining: I am not a racist.
I don't see color. I judge people by their character.

The issue of bargaining for the White Interracialist community is a matter of maintaining innocence, that is, of not being perceived to be guilty of racism. This fear of guilt prompts the familiar mantra: "I don't see color." Though this is blatantly not true, which is said to underscore one's social Innocence of racism.

The racial bargaining behind the "color-blind" response is explored in *Racism without Racists* by Eduardo Bonilla-Silva.

"Most whites assert they "don't see any color, just people";
it (race) is no longer the central factor determining minorities'
life chances...

But regardless whites' "sincere fictions," racial considerations
shade almost everything in America. Blacks and dark-skinned
racial minorities are well behind whites in virtually every area of
social life; they are about three times more likely to be poor than
whites, earn about 40 percent less than whites, and have about an
eighth of the net worth than whites have...Finally, (this is) their

overrepresentation among those arrested, prosecuted, incarcerated, and if charged with a capital crime, executed."[6]

Bonilla-Silva sees "color-blind racism" as the enigma of contemporary America. This is a form of racial dysfunction assumes a moral high ground of social innocence by closing one eye to the history of racial injustice; while allowing the other eye to locate "people of color" to which their catalog of racial faults and shortcomings can be targeted.

Joseph Barnt, a leading in anti-racism education today, sees room for the claim of innocence through ignorance in the context of the white interracialist community.

Does "white racism" mean that every white person is racist? Yes, every white person is part of the problem, but not necessarily with personal racist intent. We are assuming that most white Americans do not want to be racist. Every white person participates in and benefits from the system of racism, even if it is against our will.[7]

Whether pursuing social innocence or protected by social ignorance, color-blindness is the most common response of racial bargaining in the White interracialist community.

Racial bargaining in the Interracialist community is the attempt to live with the privileges of the status quo without responsibility for the privileges of the status quo without responsibility for the privileges are bestowed or maintained. Kovel in, *White Racism: A Psychohistory*, narrates the historical bargaining process of the White community to maintain control over Nonwhites in the United States.

The first stage he describes as "domination" in which the White community controlled Nonwhites. When this form of White supremacy was no longer possible or acceptable, the status quo of race relations became one of "separate but equal" or unequal in most cases, i.e., reservations and Jim Crow segregation for Nonwhites. In this context white supremacy is maintained through social institutions that have the power to continuously regulate, amend and correct various aspects of society. Kovel concludes that the continuance of racism is through a dynamically changing process he calls "metaracism." Metaracism is the changing face of racism. "Color-blind racism" represents a contemporary form of metaracism that allows social innocence of racial bargaining, while at the same time supporting the status quo.

Nonwhite Response to Bargaining in White Supremacy Culture

Nonwhite Interracialist Bargaining: I am not like the rest of my race, i.e., Oreo (Black), Apple (Native), Coconut (Hispanic), Banana (Asian)

Bargaining for the Nonwhite communities of origin is an effort to overcome the racism of society by "going along to get along" in order to become enfranchised into the status quo. Racial bargaining is used to move a person or people from the margins of a white supremacy culture into the mainstream. Marginalization is the exclusion of a group of people from the major resources of a community and their placement on the 'edges' of a secure and meaningful lifestyle.

In presentations and workshops in the United States, South America, Africa and Europe, I have become aware of many incidents of bargaining by Nonwhites in white supremacy cultures. Through listening to and facilitating groups, I have learned that each Nonwhite community has a descriptive term about those members of its community who are perceived as bargaining away an important element of their group bonding. In the U.S. Nonwhite communities various names used to describe members who are bargaining with the white supremacy culture. These names indicate that the individuals have internalized the white supremacy culture in a way that is shunned by their respective Nonwhite community of origin. In the Black commuity those who show conduct themselves in this way are sometimes referred to as "Oreos, black on the outside but white on the inside." In the Native American community this group is sometimes referred to as "Apples, red on the outside but white on the inside." In this Hispanic/Latino community, one of the terms used is, "Coconut, brown on the outside but white on the inside." While in the Asian community, a popular term is, "Banana, yellow on the outside but white on the inside." The descriptions of the inside indicate behaviors that are not considered part of their respective racial group, but that of the white racial culture.

These descriptions of racial bargaining from various Nonwhite communities reflect the nature of oppression as colluding in one's own victimization. To advance in an oppressive society, Nonwhite racial bargaining has also been a resource for "double consciousness" as W.E.B. Dubois noted over a century ago in his classic work, *The Souls of Black Folk*.

...the Negro... in this American world, —a world which yields him no true self-consciousness, but only lets him see himself through the revelation of the other world. It is a peculiar sensation, this double-consciousness, this sense of always looking at oneself through the eyes of others, of measuring one's soul by the tape of a world that looks on in amused contempt and pity. One feels his two-ness, —an American, a Negro; two souls, two thoughts, two unreconciled strivings; two warring ideals in one dark body, whose dogged strength alone keeps it from being torn asunder.[8]

The "double consciousness" developed by Nonwhites in our society is the product of two competing goals; survival in the face of oppression and the pervevering hope of social advancement. The development of "double consciousness" is a resource to other groups of Nonwhites in our society whether Hispanic/ Latino,[9] Asian,[10] Black[11] or new immigrants from the global community.[12]

The global dynamics of racial dysfunction in regard to racial bargaining are illuminated by Frantz Fanon, a psychiatrist from the Caribbean island of Martinique in his book, *Black Skin, White Mask*. "All forms of exploitation are identical because all of them are applied against the same 'object': man... Colonial racism is no different from any other racism."[13] He cites some of his experiences with French speaking people of African descent throughout the world. The examples are of the use of language as a tool for bargaining to gain access to the resources within a white supremacy culture. The aim of bargaining by command of the language serves to demonstrate to others that one is an exceptional Nonwhite, to be distinguished from other Nonwhites.

Yes, I must take great pains with my speech, because I shall be more or less judged by it. With great contempt they will say of me, "He doesn't even know how to speak French".

In any group of young men in the Antilles, the one who expresses himself well, who has mastered the language, is inordinately feared; keep an eye on that one, he is almost white. In France one says, "He talks like a book." In Martinique, "He talks like a white man".[14]

Racial bargaining to advance one's opportunities in a society is an issue for Nonwhites and Whites alike in our culture. However, the issue for Nonwhite Interracialists often is centered around the degree of their internalization of the status quo in relation to other members of their community of origin.

The advantage of internalization of the white status quo also applies to the external degree of whiteness. The lighter skin is a passport to upward social mobility when utilized in racial bargaining. However, the individual does not have to intentionally take advantage of the value of their complexion; others can see its value in relationship to the status quo. This can open doors that are closed to others with darker complexions in this country and throughout the world. In the ground-breaking book, *The Color Complex*, a team of authors present the value of lighter skin in the white supremacy culture of the U.S..

In 1990, sociologists Michael Hughes and Bradley Hertel examined whether skin color *per se* had any influence on the earning potential for Black Americans...To their astonishment, Hughes and Hertel also discovered that the ratio of difference in earnings between the light-skinned and the dark-skinned Blacks was proportional to that between Whites and Blacks. For every 72 cents a dark-skinned person made, a light-skinned Black earned a dollar. Even, today, it appears that Blacks with the lightest skin color have the best chances for success.[15]

Nonwhite racial bargaining strategies, such as the bleaching of dark skin, marrying lighter mates, surgical alterations of ethnic features, change of speaking patterns, change of names, etc., seek to attain greater enfranchisement a society dominated by racial caste interactions.

Nonwhite Supremacist Bargaining

Nonwhite Supremacist Bargaining: Separation from
White control of the Nonwhite community and psyche

Just as White supremacists seek to save their "whiteness" by distancing themselves from Nonwhites through seeking states and communities for "Whites only"; the Nonwhite supremacists seek an environment that is free of white controls. As the White supremacist desires to build a social space in which Nonwhites are absent, so too the Nonwhite supremacist mirrors this desire to provide a social space exclusive to their community and its institutions.

An example of a nonwhite supremacy dynamic is the efforts of some Black nationalists to move from under the burden of white power to realize black Power. As Fanon critiqued the French-speaking Black consciousness movement of the Caribbean, he has noted that the movement to blackness (Afrocentrism) was a reaction to that of whiteness (Eurocentrism) in the dominant white supremacy culture. According to Fanon, racial bargaining will have to move from its extremes of being exclusively white or exclusively black to a new point. This new point that Fanon project is a movement away from being persons defined by color (White or Nonwhite) to being defined as a "human being."

Colorist/Intermediate Response
to Bargaining in White Supremacy Culture

Colorist/Intermediate Bargaining: To escape the oppression - I
am not Nonwhite but only partially so

The racial bargaining for the Colorist/Intermediate is an attempt to find more access to social enfranchisement by being more white or less nonwhite.

The Colorist experience in the Anglo culture of the U.S. mirrors the same bargaining dynamics of the Latin culture of Central and South America. The Colorist community seek to present themselves as white people, despite the argument of the status quo with Whites and Nonwhites become fraught with private and public turmoil.

This is also the case for the Intermediate community, which are those who have white skin but have not yet been accepted into the status quo of whiteness. Their racial bargaining is an appeal to having themselves seen as "white enough" for membership into the status quo. The racial bargaining of the Intermediate community is to present the white face of their heritage, unlike the Colorist community whose effort is to cover up the nonwhite past of their heritage. However, the internal dynamic of their effort have the same force in the society, it upholds and reinforces the white supremacy culture with new actors and new energies at the expense of the Nonwhite communities.

David R. Roediger, a scholar in Critical White Studies, presents a new development in the study of how various European national groups made it into the white status quo in his book, *Working Toward Whiteness: How America's Immigrants Became White*. Roediger opens his discussion on the racification history of the U.S. with a quote by the poetess, Diane Di Prima. The racial bargaining of the Intermediate community is pointantly captured.

> *This pseudo "white" identity...was not something that just fell on us out of the blue, but something that many Italian Americans grabbed at with both hands. Many felt that their culture, language, food, songs, music, identity, was a small price to pay for entering the American mainstream. Or they thought, as my parents probably did, that they could keep these good Italian things in private and become "white" in public.[16]*

Roediger describes the pursuit of enfranchisement in the Anglo white supremacy culture at the expense of one's nowhite ethnic markings as "inbetweenness." He observes this experience as the core experience of the immigrants from Europe for the last 120 years.

Conclusion on Bargaining

The means and strategies of racial bargaining in the context of white supremacy culture can be seen in the various communities of origin. Each community has its own issue in the state of ongoing bargaining which continues throughout people's life. Bargaining is colluding with white supremacy culture to gain power, material success and prestige in a society dominated by racial caste interactions.

1 An interview with Nozipho Mfeka found on the web site, "Black Men in America." http://www.blackmeninamerica.com/coffee.htm. More about Mfeka can be found at http://www.modelsmodeling.com/portfolios/noziphomfeka-beauty/bio.htm.

2 Senna, D. (1998). The Mulatto Millennium: Where Will a Former Black Girl Fit? *Utne Reader.* September-October. 31-34.

3 Terkel, S. (1992). *Race: How Blacks and Whites Think and Feel about the American Obsession.* New York: The New Press. 272.

4 Betances, S. (1993). *African-Americans and Hispanic/Latinos: Eliminating Barriers to Coalition Building.* The Urban League of Greater Hartford , Inc., Hartford, CT, The Urban League of Greater Hartford, Inc.; for Brazilian context of bargaining refer to Robinson, E. (1999). *Coal to Cream: A Black Man's Journey Beyond Color to an Affirmation of Race.* New York, Free Press: Simon and Shuster.

5 Daniels, R. (2002). *Coming to America: A History of Immigration and Ethnicity in American Life* (2nd Edition). New York: Perennial/HarperCollins Publishers. 109-10.

6 Bonilla-Silva, E. (2006). *Racisim without Racists: Color-Blind Racism and the Persistence of Racial Inequality in the United States.* New York, Rowman & Littlefield Publishers, Inc. 1-2.

7 Barndt, J. (1991). *Dismantling Racism: The Continuing Challenge to White America.* Minneapolis, Augsburg Fortress Publisher. 35.

8 DuBois, W. E. B. (1990). *The Souls of Black Folks.* New York: Vintage Books. 8-9.

9 Rodriguez, R. (1982). *Hunger of Memory: The Education of Richard Rodriguez, An Autobiography.* New York: Bantam Windstone.; Abalos, D. T. (1986). *Latinos in the United States: The Sacred and the Political.* Notre Dame, IN: University of Notre Dame Press.; Freire, P. (1989). *Pedagogy of the Oppressed.* New York: Continuum.

10 Delgado, R., Ed. (1995). *Critical Race Theory: The Cutting Edge.* Philidelphia, Temple University Press.; Lee, J. (1997). *Performing Asian America: Race and Ethnicity on the Contemporary Stage.* Philadelphia, Temple University Press.; Featherstone, E., Ed. (1994). *Skin Deep: Women Writing on Color, Culture, and Identity.* Freedom California, The Crossing Press.

11 Fanon, F. (1963). *The Wretched of the Earth.* New York: Grove Press, Inc.; Fanon, F. (1967). *Black Skin, White Mask.* New York: Grove Press.; Betances, S. (1993). *African-Americans and Hispanic/Latinos: Eliminating Barriers to Coalition Building.* The Urban League of Greater Hartford , Inc., Hartford, CT, The Urban League of Greater Hartford, Inc.

12 Memmi, A. (1965). *The Colonizer and the Colonized.* Boston, Beacon Press.; Essed, P. (1991). *Understanding Everyday Racism: An Interdisciplinary Theory.* Newbury Park, CA, Sage Publications.; Gioseffi, D., Ed. (1993). *On Prejudice: A Global Perspective.* New York: Anchor Books.;

13 Fanon, F. (1967). *Black Skin, White Mask.* New York: Grove Press. 89.

14 Ibid. Fanon 1967: 20-21.

15 Russell, K., M. Wilson, et al. (1992). *The Color Complex: The Politics of Skin Color Among African Americans.* New York, Harcourt Brace Jovanovich. 38.

16 Roediger.R.C. (2005). *Working Toward Whiteness: How America's Immigrants*

Depression

Depression in the Recovery from Racisms™ process is understood from the perspective of the work of Dr. Elisabeth Kubler-Ross. "There are two types of depression. One is "reactive depression" a negative response to loss and the parting with fond past experiences. The second is "preparatory depression" a response that is looking forward. The first, the "reactive depression" is saying, "I don't want to be bothered," in my powerlessness of loss. The second is saying, "I don't know what to do now" in the purposefulness of life. The first is a grieving over the past; the other is a groping for the future."[1]

Voices of Depression

At the "Racism" workshop in 1999, I realized that I had viewed all my black students over my 25 years of teaching with one assumption. I treated them as though they were not equal to the white students academically, nor as gifted as the white students. Consequently, when looking for students to be in academic contests, I overlooked the African American students who, with some coaching, could have developed into good competitors. There were a couple of African American students who stood out over the years and I asked them to be involved, but I missed so many others. When I realized this I began to cry. I felt very down and depressed that I had lived such a racist view for so many years of my life. Moreover, I was saddened that what I believed I was trying to do in the ministry of education was in many ways the opposite of what I was doing. How could I have lumped so many unique and wonderful students into the same image? What a total injustice! I felt at that workshop the onset of depression. I was confronted by my racism. It depressed me – in fact, it still does.

– White male

~•~

For several years where I was a local pastor, I frequently visited the central offices of the diocese. Most often, I wore the clerical collar and did not have any problems entering the building or the cathedral church. One afternoon when I was in the area on other business, I decided to visit the cathedral. To my surprise, a security guard met me at the door and wanted me to show my credentials in order to enter. He had been instructed, I learned later, to keep the "street people" from bothering church visitors. He assumed that black single men were all out to disturb other church goers. I was furious. I wondered: how many times have I been here, led services here, preached in this place, but this day, since I did not have a collar on, I was assumed to be poor and a beggar because I was black. For several days, I was very down because of this.

When I scrutinized my soul about the depression, I realized that for many white people, even in the Church, skin color matters more than the person inside. My depression was deep because I had to face the institutionalized racism within my church. I had desired to believe that the church was different than other places. But it was not so.

– Black male

Personal Examination

Unaware

Have I ever felt helpless or hopeless in a racial situation?

Aware

Have I experienced racial depression over my powerlessness in the situation?

Self Aware

When feeling bad about a racial situation how do I move beyond racial depression?

The Depression Stage

The fourth stage of recovery is that of depression. Although there are as many definitions of depression as there are depressed people, this work utilizes the word "depression" in the classical sense of anger turned against oneself. The intervention needed in these incidents for recovery must take into account that the inward explosion of anger has as much power and effect as the outward explosion of anger. This inward explosion of anger against the self takes energy from life's activities and focuses it on the self with a heaviness of heart. In effect depression is a "wake up" call for the person to look within and to take account of themselves and their actions. Because of the negative feeling and heaviness of this state, depression is a prison whose key is insight.[1] The weakness felt in a state of depression is the result of psychic energy being drained. It requires much emotional energy to review past failures, which results in generating anxiety and dread about the future.. Dr. Kubler-Ross describes the dynamic between depression's two faces.

There are two types of depression. One is "reactive depression" a negative response to loss and the parting with fond past experiences. The second is "preparatory depression" a response that is looking forward. The first, the "reactive depression" is saying, "I don't want to be bothered," in my powerlessness of loss. The second is saying, "I don't know what to do now" in the purposefulness of life. The first is a grieving over the past; the other is a groping for the future.[2]

The grieving issue of racial depression in the Recovery from Racisms™ approach lies in failed efforts to collude with the white supremacy culture. The "reactive depression" is accompanied by a loss of self-esteem. The "preparatory depression" which is common to recovery from substance abuse and other addictive behaviors, raises the question: What will the future be without the feeling I get from my 'fix'? The question for those dealing with the racial depression becomes: What will my future be without my racial illusion?

White Response of Depression in White Supremacy Culture

White Supremacist Depression: Nonwhites are seen enjoying the benefits of White enfranchisement

The scenario for this particular community of origin is "reactive depression." A bout of "reactive depression" can be tiggered when one's privileged status is compromised. It is a feeling of powerlessness to protect the value of "whiteness." The idea of Nonwhites enjoying enfranchisement calls into question the self-esteem of their place in the national community. It is a reaction to outside circumstances that set into motion a questioning of the social order that allows such upheavals in the social order. It calls into question the unity of the "White race" to allow such a question to happen. The turmoil of the inner life is a reflection of the outer changes of the assumed social order in which the individual has a special place.

White Interracialist Depression: Discovery of racial dysfunction in attitudes, feelings and actions

Personal turmoil is also a sign of the racial depression issue for the White Interracialist. The depression emerges from a situation in which feelings, thoughts, or actions betray a desire to be free of prejudice, discrimination and racism. Reactive depression for the White Interracialist emerges from a desire to be free of racial dysfunction in their lives. The context for reactive depression can occur in the White or Nonwhite community. The individual can suffer a bout of reactive depression when shunned by Whites for their association with Nonwhites. Likewise, there can be a loss of self-esteem coming from their Nonwhite associates when their unguarded thoughts, initial reactions or social mistakes are called into question. The loss of one's valued self-image from whatever sources is a trigger for reactive depression as a "good person" or a "good White person."

In terms of a "reactive depression" there is a realization of lost social innocence as in the racial anger stage. In anger the assault on the one's self-esteem is turned outwards rather than inwards. This depression can keep the person paralyzed due to guilt feelings and a sense of powerlessness to maintain their integrity as they struggle to recover from racisms. The struggle to maintain one's racial sobriety will move the person forward to a "preparatory depression" as it prompts the person to find a strategy for their relief of guilt and way to freedom. Barndt spoke to this crippling guilt of the depression stage that can overtake White interracialists.

Dealing with our racism does not mean allowing ourselves to become puppets controlled by our guilt-strings. The alternative to racism is freedom, not another kind of slavery. Too many people never get beyond the question of guilt. Guilt is among the most ineffective motivations for positive human action. The only purpose of guilt, according to Christian teaching, is to drive us to seek forgiveness. The guilt-laden person just wallows in guilt. The forgiven person is freed to act.[3]

Seeking recovery from racisms moves the person beyond the prison of depression's guilt into realizing that our communities of origin tapes will forever play in our heads, over and over again. The intervention of recovery from racisms stops the messages of our previous tapes in order to record over the old messages. New messages from our voice of racial sobriety redirect our depression moments by calling us to move from remorse to recovery. As guilt is the emotional glue that keeps us stuck in our place, preparatory depression is a moment that gets us unstuck.

Nonwhite Response to Depression in White Supremacy Culture

Nonwhite Interracialist Depression: No guarantee of equal treatment, kept in their place

The racial depression of the Nonwhite community is well illustrated in the oldest and most oppressed communities of origin, the Native American and the Black communities. An indicator of the depressed state of the Nonwhite community is the plight of large urban areas where legal and illegal drug and alcohol sales soar. These drugs are utilized to induce an altered state of consciousness as a strategy to cope with chronic depression from one generation to the next. Beyond the urban indicator, the Native American community living on reservations finds these problems multiplied. The Indian Health Service says that for every 1,000 children born on the reservation in the late 1980's, 29 died in infancy, almost three times the national average. Death from heart disease, pneumonia, influenza and suicide was twice the national rate; from adult diabetes, four times; from alcoholism, 10 times.[4]

Racial reactive depression has become a chronic condition in many Nonwhite communities. The power of the white supremacy culture in the United States makes these oppressed communities Emergency Wards of psychic pain whose streets are the wards for the walking wounded. Though this picture is painted nightly in the electronic media and at dawn in the print media, the impression is given that this depression is limited to the Nonwhites in the underclass of our society. Ellis Cose closed his book *The Rage of a Privileged Class* commenting on the pain of a "reactive depression" affecting the Black middle class.

The pain of the professionals profiled in the preceding pages is more often than not rooted in feelings of exclusion. In attempting to escape that pain, some blacks end up, in effect, inviting increased isolation. When the successful black lawyer declares that he will "go to my own people for acceptance" because he no longer expects approbation from whites, he is not only expressing solidarity with other members of his race, he is also conceding

*defeat. He is saying that he is giving up hope of ever being any-
thing but a talented "nigger" to many of his white colleagues,
that he refuses to invest emotionally in those who will never quite
see him as one of them, whatever his personal and professional
attributes.*[5]

Racial reactive depression has become a chronic condition
in many Nonwhite communities. The chronic depression of the
Black community as it copes with the white supremacy culture has
given the world an original art form, "the Blues." The lyrics speak
to the plight of Nonwhites as living without hope of escaping a
lifelong sentence in the racial caste system, a life journey full of
disappointments from the cradle to the crypt. For members of the
Nonwhite community, the incidence of depression will make this
stage an address that is frequently visited.

*Nonwhite Supremacist Depression: The realization
that Nonwhites are bound to white society*

The realization that Nonwhite people's history, past and present, is bound up with those who are White is the issue of depression for the Nonwhite supremacist. Historically, the Nonwhite
supremacist focus was to separate the Nonwhite community from
the White community. The strategy is to free the community from
its oppressed situation. However, the five hundred year history
of racial castes in this hemisphere demonstrates the impossibility
of the task politically, economically, physically, spiritually and
psychologically. Today it is impossible to sustain such a community in a world in which globalization links every group in so
many ways.

To add to this, many people have adopted the white supremacy
cultures' values. Historically, it is the same paradigm shift that
can be seen in the story of the Exodus in the Bible. In the Old
Testament the newly freed chosen people under Moses find that
after 400 years of captivity they were more Egyptian than they
were anything else. The wandering in the desert was a time of
formation. In this formation they searched for a future of promise,
died to their oppressed psyche and gave birth to a newly formed
community of intention. This biblical hope is the hope of the

Nonwhite supremacist. When the inevitable appearance of the oppressive master's print is seen in the life of the community, there is a realization that the journey to the Promised Land free of white supremacy is an endless one. The problem with the biblical journey is that along the way the oppressed of Egypt would move into a Promised Land and become the oppressors of the Canaanites, Jebusites, the Amorites. The chosen had adopted the mindset of the oppressor and became oppressors themselves. Unfortunately, this is the tragedy of the Nonwhite supremacist for it is an internalization of the oppressor's model of peoplehood based on nationhood. In this analogy the same can be said of the White supremacists who see themselves as the chosen people, and seek a Promised Land – free of Nonwhites. Again, the example is of both forms of supremacy being mirrors of one another.

Colorist/Intermediate Response to Depression in White Supremacy Culture

Colorist Depression: Society does not let one escape their nonwhite status

Richard Rodriguez, in his autobiography *Hunger of Memory* recalls people throughout the world questioning him about his ethnic background.

Visiting the East Coast or the gray capitals of Europe during the long months of winter, I often meet people at deluxe hotels who comment on my complexion (In such hotels it appears nowadays a mark of leisure and wealth to have a complexion like mine.) Have I been skiing? In the Swiss Alps? Have I just returned from a Caribbean vacation? No. I say not softly but in a firm voice that intends to explain: My complexion is dark. (My skin is brown. More exactly, terra-cotta in sunlight, tawny in shade. I do not redden in sunlight. Instead, my skin becomes progressively dark; the sun singes the flesh.) [6]

People wonder what ethnic group many Hispanics/Latinos, Europeans, Arabs and others belong to since by "ethnic markers" they could be interchangeable with other ethnics. Nonetheless, people inquire and challenge others to identify themselves when they cannot be identified by common racial and ethnic indicators.

People's inquiries often lead to identifying where the person fits in the racial caste hierarchy. Nonwhites are seen as having less to offer in the social exchange process, ranging from the brief civilities of a passing conversation to the possibilities of dating, marriage and family life.[7]

The racial depression issue for the Colorist/Intermediate begins with the interruption of their life's pursuit because people can not escape the ongoing disenfranchisement of the Nonwhite members of a society. In Jacobson's book *Whiteness of a Different Color: European Immigrants and the Alchemy of Race* he presents a passage from Phillip Roth's *Counterlife* in which a woman rejects the shows of affection by a Jewish man because she believes he is Nonwhite.

"It is a racial matter," she insisted.

"No, we're the same race. You're thinking of Eskimos."

"We are not the same race. Not according to anthropologists, or whoever measures these things. There's Caucasian, Semitic-there are about five different groups. Don't look at me like that."

"But I am Caucasian, kiddo. In the United States census I am, for good or bad, counted as Caucasian."

"Are you? Am I wrong?"[8]

This exchange highlights a shared incident of denial in the Colorist/Intermediate sense of nonwhiteness, and denial in the White Interracialist community. The Jewish man is confronted with the common notions of race and though they are fiction, he denies his nonwhiteness. In the Colorist/Intermediate response the motivation is to gain access to the benefits of society that comes in the form of social acceptance followed by success in one's life pursuits. At the same time this conversation shows the ongoing struggle of those who have white status. Their privilege is realized in the fiction of a white identity that is tied to their collusion with the fiction of a nonwhite identity. Without the weight of the nonwhite identity there would be no value in a white identity. Maintaining white privilege commits the members of the society to do their part in policing who is enfranchised with white status and who is not.

Jacobson stresses in his work the vague nature of the racial fictions. He acknowledges that though race is a fiction, racism is a fact. To sustain the fiction of race requires the members of society to collude with the white supremacy culture so as to regulate the racial caste hiearchy.

Conclusion on Depression

Each community has its issue of depression. A "reactive depression" can be fleeting due to a specific situation that lasts a day. Or "reactive depression" can be a chronic community condition that continues on through generations. But no matter where racial depression occurs or what community it visits, the psychic energy wasted is tremendous. Both the White and Nonwhite communities suffer racial depression as a symptom of our cultural experience of racisms.

In the Nonwhite community a new "growth industry" is being built from racial depression. Our prison industry is the largest in the world. In the Nonwhite community even homes have become prisons with barred windows to protect people from their neighbors. With streets as emergency wards, homes have become infirmaries and women have become nurses to their families.

In the White community racial depression is seen in new forms disguised as "donor fatigue" and "compassion fatigue." Intervening in the depression stage can move both the nonwhite and white communities towards a more hopeful future. The key of insight can release our various communities from the prisons of depression. Release from depression in our communities can trigger a release of much needed energies that can be directed towards change. The Million Man March witnessed the tapping of these energies in the Nonwhite community in a way that excited millions and mobilized a community for action. There is life beyond depression when we accept our responsibility to become the change that we want to see. The self directed anger of depression can become changed into the energy to make a difference for one's self and those around us.

1 Kubler-Ross, E. (1973). *On Death and Dying.* New York: Macmillan Company.
2 Ibid. Kubler-Ross 1973. 76.
3 Barndt, J. (1991). *Dismantling Racism: The Continuing Challenge to White America.* Minneapolis, Augsburg Fortress Publisher. 44.
4 Kilborn, P. T. (1992). Sad Distinction for the Sioux: Homeland is No. 1 in Poverty. *The New York Times.* New York.
5 Cose, E. (1993). *The Rage of a Privileged Class.* New York: HarperCollins Publishers. 188.
6 Rodriguez, R. (1982). *Hunger of Memory: The Education of Richard Rodriguez, An Autobiography.* New York, Bantam Windstone. 113.
7 Russell, K., M. Wilson, et al. (1992). *The Color Complex: The Politics of Skin Color Among African Americans.* New York, Harcourt Brace Jovanovich.
8 Jacobson, M. (1998). *Whiteness of a Different Color: European Immigrants and the Alchemy of Race.* Cambridge, MA: Harvard University Press.

Acceptance

Acceptance begins with the acknowledgement of one's racial dysfunction and ends with a commitment to the healing journey towards racial sobriety.

Voices of Acceptance

In my town, the younger school-aged children hang out at a local gas station/store before and after school, as well as on Friday nights after ballgames. When it was the Black children congregating, the issue was addressed by the local police patrolling the area to keep down the number of youth and the noise. The result of this patrolling caused the number of Blacks to stop hanging around the location after a few run-ins with the law. In a turn of events, the same location is now frequented by groups of Whites with the same behavior that the Black youth exhibited. You cannot even get into the parking lot on Friday nights. It is expected that if the Blacks are there in large numbers and not moving, the law will be contacted; but not if it is a white crowd. Blacks have to be prepared to shop and spend their money, but monitor the time spent in one place otherwise they will be policed.

This situation for me is a realization of acceptance. Black people, wherever they find themselves, are in a hostile environment in this country.

– Black female

~•~

The illusion that I gave up a long time ago is that of thinking I could never be racist because I am brown. Memory has shown me that I was brought-up in a racist environment feeling sorry for those who had less, being careful about who I played with, seeing my father fight with the Black neighbor, hearing that some Blacks are better than others and being ashamed of my Mexican heritage (Mexican did not mean being brown; it meant being non-documented, uneducated migrant). The illusion was that if I hung around with other Hispanics who fit into a white way of being I would be accepted. This was not hard to accomplish; all I had to say was that I did not grow-up speaking Spanish, implying that I was more white (acceptable to "Anglos") than brown. I now realize that this was common among second and third generation Hispanics.

Acceptance was challenging because I did not know what it meant to be discriminated against; I denied that I had ever experienced it, as did others like me. To admit that I was discriminated against meant that I was "other" and this was bad. This denial is no longer part of my self-realization or collective identity. I now realize what it means to celebrate my heritage: do it the best I can and delight in those moments.

– Hispanic/Latino male

~•~

In a miscommunication about mutual expectations, I found myself at odds with an African American female colleague of mine. It was a very perplexing situation because I thought I was right and she was wrong. After a long while of this emotional turmoil, I came to a realization. The inner conflict and emotional turmoil indicated that I needed to accept the fact that my racial attitudes and stereotypes were very much a part of my psyche. And try as I might not to act as a racist nor speak like a racist, I still had those feelings and attitudes ingrained in me from my culture, from my social context.

It was from my own emotional turmoil around this conflict with someone with whom I worked so well that I began to see my relationship with other African American women followed a similar pattern. I had to accept that this is a part of what it means to be White. My recovery from this position was to accept my reality and to admit who I am, observe how I play it out, and work to change myself.

– White male

~•~

It wasn't until I began my own work in recovery that I realized two things – even as a White woman of moderate income (working poor) I still have White privilege in that I indirectly benefit from being White in spite of my socio-economic level – also that I have been a victim of the White male dominated culture. These realizations were a shock. However, moving through them has strengthened my resolve to continue to work on my own recovery and help others.

– White female

Personal Examination

Unaware

Am I aware of insights I have gained in regard to racial acceptance?

Aware

What does my acceptance challenge me to do?

Self Aware

What difference will my racial acceptance make in my life? And in the life of others?

The Acceptance Stage

The fifth stage is that of acceptance, and it is the final stage in the Kubler-Ross model. The Kubler-Ross model would end in the death of the patient from a terminal illness. In the acceptance stage, the patient accepts that death is near. The Linn Brothers' model of "healing life's hurts" interprets the acceptance stage as a choice to live in the present and to let go of past hurts. Kubler-Ross reflected on this stage as a time to recollect oneself in order to call on inner strength for a daunting task ahead.

Acceptance should not be mistaken for a happy stage. It is almost void of feelings. It is as if the pain had gone, the struggle is over, and there comes a time for "the final rest before the long journey" as one patient phrased it.[1]

The "recovery from everyday racisms" process interprets racial acceptance as the stage in which a decision is made and emotional resources are found to make the commitment to racial sobriety. The acceptance stage is a "commencement event." A series of new learnings, moral inventories and soulful wrestling have come to an end. Now it is time for the "life" after learning to begin, a lifestyle of racial sobriety. Racial acceptance announces the commencement of the sober self and the death of the racialized self. In the dying process of the racialized self the emergence of the sober self challenges our being in the world. A shift occurs from the Don't Rules of race relations to the Do Rules of racial sobriety. The Do Rules allow a person to talk about racial dysfunction, to feel the tensions of racisms and to trust one's sober self as we build new relationships in the human family.

White Response to Acceptance of White Supremacy

White Supremacist Acceptance: The value of society's enfranchisement is based on my humanity not my whiteness

The "long journey" for the White supremacist is to accept every person including themselves as a valued human being regardless of race. The White psychiatrist Kovel spoke of a journey to the heart of the reality of recovery in a white supremacy culture.

To go beyond racism genuinely means at the bottom that the other is considered a human, not a thing, he may be a lovable human, he may be an unlovable human, or he may be, like most humans, an amazing mixture of strengths and weaknesses, assets and deficits, lovable and unlovable traits, all bound up in various conflicts. In a free, non-racist culture, one grants an intrinsic worth to the other person, simply because he is human; this does not mean however, that one must love him.[2]

For the White supremacist to accept that one is worthy of respect because of their humanity allows that person to experience a sense of self-esteem based on another value other than "whiteness." Acceptance can establish a ground of being "beyond" our racial identity formation. It is the goal of New Family Formation in support groups to take us "beyond" the fiction of race to the deeper reality of the human family.

White Interracialist Acceptance: My recovery from racisms begins within myself and my world

The "long journey" for White interracialists is to accept their racial dysfunction from its formation in their community of origin to its everyday manifestations. The decision-making and calling forth of one's emotional resources means that acceptance is not a single declaration. It is an ongoing task that calls for an ever deepening deliberation on what a commitment to racial sobriety requires. James Barndt and Charles Ruehle in an article "Rediscovering a Heritage Lost: A European-American Anti-racist

Identity" witness to their journey of acceptance.

For most White Americans, an initial reaction to the realization of white racism is either a debilitating guilt or the pretense that one can become a non-racist. We can become travelers on the road to a new white cultural identity only when we are able to accept the reality of our racist identity and begin to participate in collective efforts to combat and dismantle.[3]

Acceptance becomes an exit door from a lifestyle of "stinking thinking" and an entrance way to becoming a fully functioning human being. Dying to the racialized self and its participation in the white supremacy culture releases toxic emotional energies and redirects them for use in constructing a culture of racial sobriety.

Nonwhite Response to Acceptance of White Supremacy
Nonwhite Interracialist Acceptance:
Acceptance of operating in a hostile society

The "long journey" of the Nonwhite Interracialist in the Americas can be seen as the biblical journey through the desert to the Promised Land. It is a terrain of struggle, a daily struggle for life. Nonwhites on the planet today suffer greatly due to the disease of racial dysfunction wherever they live. Due to the reach of globalization and western white supremacy Nonwhite people are being crushed to the earth everyday in the global village. Charles Mills' analysis of the globality of white supremacy in his book *The Racial Contract* frames race around the politics of power. He concludes that "White is not a color at all, but a set of power relationships."[4] In our world of white power Nonwhites racial acceptance is a life long struggle of resistance to oppression and vigilance towards new forms of dehumanization.

Racial acceptance for Nonwhites is not the calm before commitment to the struggle for racial sobriety, but the creation of a calm within the sober self to withstand the unrelenting and raging storm of racisms. Rev. Dr. Yvonne Delk of Chicago gives a personal testimony that captures the acceptance stage for the Nonwhite person.

Racism became a life-threatening reality that impacted every facet of my life. It was like an imprisoning cage destroying community, dehumanizing persons and locking Blacks and Whites alike into confrontational roles and identities. It determined what we thought and believed, how we acted and reacted, who we trusted and who we dare not trust.[5]

Accepting the hostile realities of the world around them the Nonwhite community faces multiple challenges. The hostility of the various communities, both Nonwhite, White and Intermediate/Colorist, makes the commencement of the journey an arduous daily task.

Where do people turn for support and encouragement? Many people turn to their religious centers for comfort and support. However, the hostile environment that exists in the culture is reflected in its religious institutions. The renowned Black theologian Rev. Dr. James Cone speaks to an acceptance that allows Nonwhites and Whites to begin the "long journey" to a spiritual center that will be life giving to the human family.

I now realized why it had been so difficult for me to make the connection between the black experience and theology. Racists do not define theology in a way that challenges their racism. To expect White theologians to voluntarily make theology relevant to Black peoples struggle for justice is like expecting Pharaoh in Egypt to voluntarily liberate Israelites from slavery. It is the victims and those who identify with them that must make the connection between their struggle and the gospel.[6]

Religion's reinforcement of the white supremacy culture is a part of the hostile environment of the world in which Nonwhites live. Identifying the sources of racial dysfunction frees the religious imagination to realize its own Exodus "journey" from the bondage of racisms in its pursuit of the vision of a Promised Land. Our religious affiliations have supported the racial dysfunction in our society. Nonwhites in the various religious traditions can attest to this reality. For the most part institutional religious behavior has been the bulwark for 500 years of intergenerational suffering for Nonwhites. Acceptance is the awareness that my own religious views can support racial dysfunction unless they are critiqued from the viewpoint of recovery. For Nonwhites in this hemisphere the history of the churchs' role in oppressive societies is a source of intergenerational racial dysfunction for the last 500 years.

Nonwhite Supremacist Acceptance:
Nonwhites are part of society and deserve enfranchisement

Nonwhite supremacists have chosen to build up alternative institutions in the face of white supremacy. The stage of acceptance challenges the Nonwhite supremacist to accept that we are all in relationship to one another. Part of this acceptance lies in the fact that, given the scope and power of the reach of white supremacy, there is little hope of success for a separate reality.

Catherine Meeks speaks to the challenge of acceptance in finding the issues of nonwhite supremacy in the midst of the larger community.

Our only hope is for blacks to start owning our personal darkness. Our wounds are not totally the fault of Whites. We are persons and we must accept responsibility for the lives which have been given to us. We have to struggle for wholeness just like our foreparents. We must choose between life, which involves struggle, or death.[7]

The struggle for wholeness does not necessitate that Nonwhites must be apart as communities in order to realize themselves. What limits their future are the racially dysfunctional cultural patterns and social structure of the white supremacy culture. A Nonwhite supremacy is not the answer; recovery from racisms is an acceptance that Nonwhites are called to realize another option. The journey of Malcolm X demonstrates that a Nonwhite supremacist can find him/herself, in a place in which one realizes that everyone is my sister or brother.

Colorist/Intermediate Response to Acceptance of White Supremacy

Colorist/Intermediate Acceptance: The need to recover their self-esteem based on their person not their degree of whiteness

A self-esteem based on whiteness leaves the individual in this community of origin always wanting to be more "white." Access to the benefits of our society is grounded in the dignity of the person. It is the dignity of the person that deserves enfranchisement, not the degree of "whiteness" one has due to the heritage of his/her gene pool.

Helen Zia describes the turmoil and challenge found in the Intermediate community around the issues of acceptance in her book *Asian American Dreams: The Emergence of an American People*. Zia poses a question about how a people become included. This is an ongoing issue for the ten million Asian Americans from various countries. She pursues two questions throughout her book: "What does it take to become American?" and the deeper question "What we've really been wanting to know is how to become accepted as Americans?" Zia's work is a response to a disturbing racial acceptance event. It was the 1982 murder of Vincent Chin in Detroit, Michigan. After celebrating his bachelor party with friends, there were insults addressed to his Asian group by some of the other customers. As Chin's group left the bar, a group of White men followed them outside the bar. This group beat Chin so badly that he later died. Nine months later Judge Charles Kaufman gave the two men involved probation saying, "These aren't the kind of men you send to jail." Zia recounts that the leader in Detroit's Chinatown expressed the loss of esteem for the Asian community when he lamented, "You go to jail for killing a dog." [8]

Acceptance of the issue of value for Nonwhites as full human beings in the human community and the justice system called Zia to action. Racial acceptance is not silent acceptance, but a resolve to take responsibility for one's response to racial dysfunction. The white supremacy culture has created mantras which represent its hostility towards the Nonwhite population. In the Black community a common mantra during times of economic stress is that of "the last hired, the first fired." The Native American community have been taunted with "The only good Indian is a dead Indian." And Zia reflected on the Chin murder as an affirmation of the mantra "Don't have a Chinaman's chance." This mantra refers to the lynching of Asians in California in which there was no punishment and also to the lynchings of thousands of Blacks throughout the country.

Conclusion on Acceptance

Acceptance as a stage in the healing process[9] acknowledges racial dysfunction at the personal, social and cultural levels. The work of this stage is to bring about the emergence of the sober self in place of the racialized self. The sober self moves beyond denying one's racial collusion with the culture to the examination of one's issues around racial dysfunction. It is a personal moral inventory of the affect of the "stinking thinking" of one's racial dysfunction. In racial acceptance the sober self assumes responsibility for maintaining a commitment to racial sobriety. In the end, racial acceptance does not mean we are responsible for all the racial dysfunctions within ourselves and our world. But it does mean we accept the responsibility for our response to what is happening within us, to us and in the world around us.

1 Kubler-Ross, E. (1973). *On Death and Dying.* New York: Macmillan Company. 100.

2 Kovel, J. (1970). *White Racism: A Psychohistory.* New York: Pantheon Books. 213.

3 Barndt, J. and C. Ruehle (1992). *Rediscovering a Heritage Loss : A European-American Anti-racist Identity. America's Original Sin.* B. Hulteen and J. Wallis. Washington, D. C. : *Sojourners.* 73-77.

4 Mills, C.W. (1997). *The Racial Contract.* New York, Cornell University Press. 125.

5 Barndt, J. (1991). *Dismantling Racism: The Continuing Challenge to White America.* Minneapolis, Augsburg Fortress Publisher. Preface vii.

6 Cone, J. H. (1992). My Soul Looks Back. America's Original Sin. B. Hulteen and J. Wallis. Washington, D. C., *Sojourners.* 46.

7 Meeks, C. (1992). *Rage and Reconciliation: Two Sides of the Same Coin. America's Original Sin.* B. H. J. Wallis. Washington, D. C. : *Sojourners.* 160-161.

8 Zia, H. (2000). *Asian American Dreams: The Emergence of an American People.* New York, Farrar, Straus and Giroux. 60-61.

9 Linn, D. and M. Linn (1978). *Healing Life's Hurts: Healing Memories through the Five Stages of Forgiveness.* New York: Paulist Press.

Re-engagement

Re-engagement is the stage in which we transform our thinking, feeling and acting in order to become the change we want to see. Re-engagement takes us from under the influence of our racial dysfunction. The racialized self gives way to the emergence of the sober self.

Voices of Re-engagement

I was shopping in a mall with a very good friend of mine who is a White female. She owed me $20. At the first shop we stopped in I went to the counter to purchase some cologne and before reaching it, my friend gave me the $20 she owed me. When I got to the counter the clerk said that will be $12.50 and I gave her the 20 dollar bill. When she had the change ready she was passing it to my friend, and I asked her what was she doing, she just looked funny and said, "Oh I am sorry, "I thought…" Before she could finish her statement, my friend told her "that is all right; we will shop somewhere else." She could not believe people are still like this.

— Black female

~•~

When my grandson was about 4-years old, we bought him a cowboy outfit, complete with cowboy boots and hat. One day when he was wearing his outfit, he told me that I should get cowboy boots like his. I looked at him and told him that I could not wear cowboy boots. He asked why not. I told him because I was an Indian, from a line of Mexican Indians, and we wore moccasins, not boots. He looked so bewildered. I'm sure he was thinking, Oh no; my Tata and I are on opposite sides; cowboys and Indians are always killing each other; what do we do now?"

That was a long time ago, but it opened a line of communication between us so that throughout his life we have always been able to talk about ethnicities, differences, and roots, and the appreciation thereof.

— Hispanic/Latino male

~•~

Over the past several years, I have been invited to participate in a variety of initiatives that have sought to address the issues of unemployment/underemployment among the Native people of this land. The other participants involved in these initiatives have been both Natives and non-Native. In our discussions, colonialism and paternalism were identified by many as root causes of the problem. But I pointed out in the various groups that I worked with the fact that it was racism which was the source of all the root causes that people had identified. The response to my assertion was consistently one of initial denial and indignation. In some of the groups that I worked with we were not able to proceed any further with any kind of dialogue about racism because the people in the group remained in denial.

In some of the other groups that I worked with however, it was possible to get the people in the group to take a closer look at the role of racism as it relates to the issue of the employment of Native people. The outcome was both positive and constructive once people were able to move beyond denial and deal with the issue honestly.

— Native American male

•~

I have two experiences of my own re-engagement. Working at the Community Center, I try to deal with each person that I serve as a unique individual and not as a set of stereotypes. I see that this effort is an ongoing challenge. I also attended a citywide prayer service at the town center, and joined in the "March for Non-Violence" following the civil disturbances in my city.

These, especially the latter, are concrete steps I took trying to be part of the solution to the racial injustice in my community. I see them as part of my own racial sobriety effort as I understand it.

— White male

Personal Examination

Self Aware
How will I begin my re-engagement with my life as a racially sober person?

The Re-engagement Stage

There are eight stages in the Recovery from Racisms™ approach. The first five stages are focused on stopping the "stinking thinking" of racial dysfunction. The last three stages deal with living one's racial sobriety. The first stage of racial sobriety is re-engagement. The central struggle of re-engagement is to transform the way that we participate in society. Re-engagement follows the decision to accept responsibility for becoming the change in race relations that one wants to see.

A person choosing a lifestyle of racial sobriety will be confronted by many challenges in a society that operates in a state of racial dysfunction. Though re-engagement is a personal commitment, it has its impact on those who are around the racially sober person. Writers in race relations point out that the person who addresses issues of racisms, thus breaking the "Don't Talk" Rule, is usually seen as "the problem" rather than the messenger. However, it is each person's choice on the manner and the nature of their re-engagement. An individual's re-engagement is as unique as their circumstances.

Levels of Re-engagement

Re-engagement is acting on one's acceptance of his/her issues of racial dysfunction. Acting to promote the sober self in place of the racialized self is what re-engagement is all about. Re-engagement realizes that the world of racisms will not change itself for me, but it can change because of me. Re-engagement assumes the responsibility of changing race relations from the inside out.

Beginning with my racial sobriety, I become the change that I want to see in the world around me. Re-engagement as a lifestyle will call for a new understanding of my world from the personal to the global levels. The sober self will have to change the paradigms in which it thinks of race, as well as its understanding of the social and cultural paradigms in which we live. The following chapter will review various levels in our lives as they challenge the sober self. The power of paradigms on our thinking and living is highlighted to show the unseen dynamics of culture which will challenge us in our re-engagement.

The Personal Level

Re-engagement is the placing of new lens over our eyes in order to change the way we see things. The lens of racial sobriety makes needed adjustments to our thinking, feeling and acting in regard to racial beliefs and cultural taboos. Rather than engaging life from the lens of the racialized self, the sober self emerges to inform our actions of relating to the world around us. The paradigm shift, that is, the change of view, calls for new ways of thinking about racial issues. Just as the exploration of the stages of recovery is an opportunity to change one's paradigm or viewpoint, re-engagement is living out this commitment.

Here is a communication illustration that demonstrates the power of one's paradigm to see things a certain way. This widely used illustration is shared here to make the point of the importance of one's paradigm to what we see and do not see.

Please follow the directions for this exercise.

1. Place a large dot **on** the "i" figure below.
2. Write the first four letters of your first name in the *spaces* provided.

1) I   2) — — — — —

This exercise demonstrates how we gather information into our existing paradigms. No matter what information is given to us we filter it through our paradigms. We are constantly constructing our world with unexamined paradigms. On the next page you can see what the exercise asked you to do. Did you follow the directions, or did you change the meaning of the information to make it fit into your existing paradigm? Most people do not respond to the reality of the request, but interpret the directions to fit into their preconceived paradigm.

This popular exercise captures the importance of realizing how much we use our paradigms in communicating ideas. Given the importance of our paradigm in race relations, there is a need to be more aware of what vision we are using to make a better world. As we re-engage our racial sobriety, we are taking ideas that are new to do something new. When we are in the process of re-engagement for racial sobriety, we are challenged to reflect deeply on what we are doing more so than what we are saying. We could be thinking and acting in our old paradigm of race relations when we think we are really embracing the new. In this work of re-engagement new language is important because it assists the visioning of the new paradigm in contrast to the old paradigm.

The Social Level

The social level of re-engagement is the adoption of the "Do Talk Rules," (see page 190). Re-engagement for racial sobriety finds itself in its place in the metaphor or paradigm of the dysfunctional family. It continues to find the same dynamics that are found in the dysfunctional family and applies them to the nation/family. When persons in a dysfunctional family begin to heal and move on to re-engage their lives, there is often a denial or a refusal by members who are obeying the "Don't Talk" Rule to recognize the family trauma that the recovering individual relates.[2] The recovering individuals become an object of ridicule and harassment because they refuse to continue to collude with the family taboos.

This dysfunctional family dynamic is present in the social collusion of the American family's response to racisms. Darling Villena-Mata in her book *Walking Between Winds: A Passage Through Societal Trauma and Its Healing* describes the responses of socially abused groups developed to protect themselves in a hostile culture. She points out a significant defense mechanism that supports cultural denial known as the "Don't Rules" developed by Claudia Black, Janet Woititz and others.

The "Don't Rules" are "don't feel, don't trust, and don't talk." In other words, do not feel your feelings, do not trust yourself (or others), and do not talk about the problem to others....[3]"

The "Don't Rules" allow for social interaction to continue as if nothing terrible is happening while in the background the abuses continue, (See page 190). For the abuse to continue there must be an ongoing silencing of protest with the support of social collusion. The "Don't Rules" are in force within families and in societies where there is abuse. It is this social collusion that has its cultural roots in American families in general that gave rise to the military solution surrounding gays and lesbians in the Armed Services. The policy is known in popular media as "Don't ask, don't tell."

The major work of recovery from racisms is breaking the "Don't Rules." Breaking out of denial brings about sobriety, that is being S-O-B-E-R, Seeing Others as Being Entitled to Respect. The "Don't Feel" Rule is broken when we explore our racial anger issues in order to bring about our recovery. And we break the "Don't Trust" Rule when we have confidence in ourselves to become the change we want to see. Racial sobriety moves beyond breaking the "Don't Rules" to living the "Do Rules"; that is, "Do Talk," "Do Feel," and "Do Trust." Re-engagement is trusting, talking and feeling ourselves towards racial sobriety. Just as our denial is personal, so too our re-engagement. It is the inner dialogue with ourself that characterizes the "talking" aspect of this stage. The inner dialogue of the sober self acknowledges our feeling and trusts the information that they bring to our awareness.

Re-engagement of one's social behavior begins with permission to witness to one's reality as it is seen through the paradigm of

1) ❙   2) —D—O—U—G—

racial sobriety. As people find their sober voice; the new voice, the new self begins to trust its experience. The inner dialogue is necessary to discover their own feelings around racial realities and interactions. From the trust of self through inner dialogue, the voice of the emerging new self gives confidence in the journey towards maintaining racial sobriety.

Re-engagement at the social level also calls for examining the circles that have supported racial dysfunction in one's life. Three of the most common social networks to examine are: the community of origin, the reference community, and the community of intention. The community of origin is the community in which we had our childhood formation. It is in this community that our social orientation around racial issues begins. In our present day situation, it is our community of reference that frames our racial issues. Communities we "refer to" to situate our everyday behavior include the neighborhood, the workplace and religious congregation (church, temple, mosque). These communities communicate the role that race plays with that particular "go along to get along" culture.

The community of intention describes voluntary associations that we choose to give our time, talent and treasure for the betterment of the human family. Organizations draw their membership and their staffing from society in general. The noble goals of our organizatons are compromised unless the racial dysfunction within our organizational culture is addressed. A lifestyle of racial sobriety will be challenged by our communities of origin, reference and intention. Each one of these communities can also be enriched by the challenge of our personal re-engagement journey in their midst.

Global Level

The racial caste hierarchy is the backbone of the white supremacy culture in the western hemisphere. Its cultural implantation into the foundations of the hemisphere was the consequence of the Spanish conquest of America (North, South and the Caribbean) from the 1500's to today. The most intact record of the construction of this racial hierarchy is found in the region known as New Spain which is today called the country of Mexico. The racial caste hierarchy was developed to regulate who would be recognized as members of society and who would not. At birth a person was assigned one of 16 castes with various social ranks (See pages 196-197). The racial caste in which one was born dictated the freedom of the person to enjoy full membership of the society. In the social ranking of the Mexican Castes or Las Castas Mexicanas[2], the members of the society that were Spanish were in the first rank of caste and exempt from being profiled as a racial caste at all. The Spanish were able to enter into government service, the army, hold political position and enter the seminary or convent to pursue religious leadership. The "other" members in the racial caste system – indigenous people and imported Africans were denied entry into these positions. In fact, without some mixture of Spanish (white) blood, they have limited opportunities in the society to this day. The more Spanish blood a person had in colonial Latin America, the higher their racial caste.

Upward social movement in the racial caste involved acquiring Spanish blood. The top three castes were ususally the castizo, mestizo and mulatto. The child of a mixture between a Spaniard and a criollo, a Spanish person born outside of Spain produced a castizo. The offspring of a Spanish person and an indigenous parent would produce a mestizo, or mixed offspring. The offspring of Spanish and African heritage would produce a mulatto. The Spanish blood from Spain was the valuable element even for those who were Spanish but not born in Spain. Though they were Spanish they were not white enough to escape being "casted" or castizo. Historians question the fiction of the Medieval Spanish population having pure blood given the African Moors occupying the country for over 300 years.

The cultural foundation for the racial profiling of dark-skinned people is captured in the representation of the indigenous and African people of the Spanish colonies. The need for and dread of the African presence in New Spain is reflected in their racial classification. The need for their labor can be seen in the term "mulatto," the offspring of Spanish and African parents. The word mulatto means "a mule." The dreaded aspect of the African presence was the term given to the offspring of indigenous and African parents, which is lobo. The term lobo means "a wolf." The cultural message presents the offspring of Africans as having the characteristics of animals. Other Spanish countries such as Peru developed their own racial caste hierarchy. (See page 191.)

As more European nations entered the globalization process brought on by the markets of the New World each would adopt a form of this racial caste hierarchy to rank those of privilege and those of disenfranchisement. Whether the colonizing nation was French, Portuguese, Dutch, or English, their republics today continue to suffer from the social illness of their racial castes. The racial caste hierarchy has been the source of chronic racial dysfunction in the hemisphere for the last 500 years.

The United States census bureau has adopted its own version of a racial caste hierarchy. Instead of 16 racial castes there are five. The Federal Five, as they are commonly referred to, are: White, African American, Asian, Native American/Pacific Island and Hispanic/Latino. However, the one ethnic group Hispanic/Latino is often divided into existing racial categories to re-emphasize the racial caste organization of society over the ethnic origins status. Today, 500 years after the construction of racial castes hierarchy, nations are still giving life to this fiction and new energy to its enforcement.

National Level

The Great Seal of The United States has rarely been cast for public use though it can be found on the one dollar bill. It was placed on the one dollar bill by President Franklin D. Roosevelt in 1935.[6] The Great Seal is a text that speaks to the paradigm that the nation was constructed by a group whom we now call the Founding Fathers of the country.[7] By examining the paradigm or model that the founders of the republic used one can see that we not only think in paradigms but that immigration and social participation in this culture is also done according to a cultural paradigm. As citizens we live in a cultural legacy which is based upon a paradigm. By examining this paradigm we can ask ourselves "How are we participating in this paradigm?"

In the history of social relationships this nation was founded on a social pyramid in which White Christian males with land and capital made up the governing elite in the colonial social structure. Those other than White, male, landed capitalists were politically and socially marginalized and disenfranchised in the American nation/family. To recover from the racisms of the American nation/family one needs to look at the "family secrets" to see the "original sins" and family traumas.

In the nation/family the American pyramid was to work for those who were on top. The top tier of society were those who were outside the caste of Nonwhites. They were the landed White male gentry who were often the first White supremacists of the new nation. The Founding Fathers formed an elite circle whose members were instrumental in the establishment of a secret organization called the Freemasons, which had its roots in Europe. It is in the context of their symbolic belief that the interpretation of the destiny of the nation/family would be casted. The members of the Freemasons' elite circle were given the positions of leadership in the Revolution and afterwards the positions of leadership in establishing the social, political and legal arrangements of the nation and its culture. When we examine their cultural leadership we see that our re-engagement must include a cultural dimension in order to provide a change in the paradigm of our society.

An example of the cultural influence of the Freemasons is the role of George Washington as the "Father of our Country." Washington, who is honored on the one dollar bill, was the leader of the Revolutionary Army and the first President of the Republic. The capital of the new nation has his name, "Washington, D. C." M. Howard depicted the crucial leadership role of Washington in formation of the embryonic nation.

George Washington was himself a high-ranking Mason. He had taken his first degree initiation at a lodge in Fredericksburg, Virginia in 1734. Among the fifty-six American rebels who signed the Declaration of Independence only six were not members of the Masonic Order. The majority of the military commanders of the American revolutionary army which fought the British during the War of Independence were practicing Freemasons.[8]

In depicting the cultural paradigm, there was a three man committee established: Benjamin Franklin, who appears on the Hundred Dollar bill, Thomas Jefferson, who would become a President and appears on the Twenty Dollar bill and Charles Thompson.[9] The committee submitted many images in its six years before the Egyptian landmark of the Pyramid at Gizeh was adopted by the Continental Congress. [10] The Egyptian pyramid captured the symbolic vision of the Founding Fathers.

The Great Seal has two sides; the reverse side with the Pyramid and the obverse side with the American Eagle. The Pyramid at Gizeh is symbolic of the Egyptian paradigm upon which the new nation was founded. The founders of the republic attempted to construct a new nation that would be as legendary as Egypt.[11] Those involved wanted to form their own country based upon the ancient Egyptian civilization as their paradigm for the new nation. The members who were inducted into the lodge admired 'things Egyptian.' For example, the Washington Monument is the tallest replica of an Egyptian obelisk in the world. Only a pharaoh in Egyptian times could have an obelisk erected.[12] Their love for 'things Egyptian' would find its way into the Great Seal of the United States through Charles Thompson, the designer of the reverse side of the Seal and William Barton, the designer of the obverse side of the Seal.[13]

One of the 'things Egyptian' that is part of the symbolism that comes out of the Freemason history of colonial America is the value of the number thirteen. The number thirteen, for the Egyptians and later through copying the Egyptian tradition, is a symbol of a metaphysical change or transformation from old to new.[14] This unique appreciation was limited to the initiated Freemasons. For the common citizen, the number 13 was promoted as a bad luck number. It was a number to be dreaded by the initiated members of the lodge. [15] People do not want to be on the 13th floor of a hotel, the 13th row in a plane and have a cultural superstition about 'Friday the 13th.' This reluctance to use the number 13 can be traced to the sacredness of the number by the Freemasons of colonial America. It was their sacred number. As 'freemasons' building the new pyramid of the American nation, the architects used the sacred number to make holy their work. Looking at the Great Seal, there are at least ten if not more examples of the number 13 depending on how one would count them.[16] (See page 191.)

The Obverse - Front of the Great Seal: The Pyramid

Designed by Charles Thomson

1) 13 levels of the pyramid

2) The Latin "Annuit Coeptis," 'God favors our beginning' has 13 letters

3) The Roman numeral at the base of the pyramid "MDC-CLXXVI," '1776' commemorates the birthday of the nation, July 4. This date is 13 days after the Summer Solstice (June 21) when the sun is highest in the sky.

The Reverse Side - Back of the Great Seal : The American Eagle

Designed by William Barton

4) The American Eagle with 13 stars above it's head representing the 13 colonies

5) The banner in the eagle's beak, "E Pluribus Unum," 'One out of many' has 13 letters

6) On the Eagle's shield there are 13 vertical strips

7) The Eagle's shield has 13 horizontal strips

8) In the eagles right claw, there are 13 arrows to symbolize readiness for war

9) In the eagle's left claw, the olive branch has 13 leaves. The olive branch symbolizes readiness for peace.

10) The olive branch has 13 olives

The Freemasons felt they were the chosen Elect of the Egyptian god Horus, the major god of the Egyptian trinity. Later in our nation's history this would be reflected in the change of the eye above the pyramid to the left eye of Horus rather than the right eye used in Christian depictions of God. In Egyptian mythology the god Horus had his left eye cut out by his evil brother Set. (This has a resemblance to the Cain and Abel story in the Old Testament). The Eye of Horus is believed to keep watch over the Elect of Horus. [17] The elitism of the founding cultural paradigm of the United States as the New Egypt could explain the reluctance of Congress to use The Great Seal for official purposes.

Anthony Browder's study of the cultural imitation of ancient Egypt in the founding of the country includes the unique design of Washington, D.C. He notes that the Potomac River running through the District of Columbia was seen as the new Nile. As with ancient Egypt the memorial buildings were to be on the west bank of the river representing the setting sun and the death of day. In Egypt the tombs are on the west side of the Nile in what is called the City of the Dead. The executive offices were to be on the east bank of the river, as in ancient Egypt, in which the eastside formed the City of the Living. It is an irony of history that in 200 years the 13 colonies have become the most powerful nation in the world. The cultural paradigm of the United States as the new Egypt of its day is realized.

The Great Seal of the United States as a sociotext speaks to the context of class, race and gender, the metatext of the social construction of reality in 'things Egyptians,' and the subtext of Freemason elitism. As a sociotext it details the origin of our social arrangements that would set up endless tensions in our American family. We are still as an American family suffering from the "original sin" of our nation: racism.[18]

Conclusion

In regard to personal engagement, the racially sober self is attentive to the 'Do Rule' of New Family formation. The core of re-engagement is self awareness which fosters thinking in areas that were once taboo. Self awareness is recognizing the feelings that one experiences as these feelings arise around our racial identity. These feelings are a part of our awareness of the interactions we have with others. In re-engagement we become responsible to reflect on what our feelings mean for us and our path to racial sobriety. The stress is placed on accepting what I must do for racial sobriety as opposed to what others are willing to do in our "go along to get along" society.

Re-engagement requires a shift in one's paradigm or vision for society. The Great Seal of the dollar bill of the United States is an example of one group's engagement with their paradigm or social vision. Through initiation into the Masonic lodge, they shared their vision and found group support for their paradigm. To realize its vision, engagement meant a commitment of lives and resources to support the construction of the paradigm. Just as racial sobriety uses the paradigm of the New Family formation as an initiation into seeing people as our brothers and sisters, the Founding Fathers used the pyramid of hierarchy as their paradigm vision that divides the human family into racial, gender and class groups. Racial re-engagement begins by choosing the paradigm to which we are committed. The Founding Fathers constructed their paradigm of the New Egypt. We are challenged to engage our lives and resources to support the paradigm of the New Family.

1   Essed, P. (1991). *Understanding Everyday Racism: An Interdisciplinary Theory.* Newbury Park, CA: Sage Publications.; Rutstein, N. (1993). *Healing in America: A Prescription for the Disease.* Springfield: Whitcomp Publishing.; Fine, M. (1997). Witnessing Whiteness. *Off White: Readings on Race, Power and Society.* Ed. M. Fine. New York: Routledge.

2   LaMar, D. F. (1992). *Transcending Turmoil: Survivors of Dysfunctional Families.* New York: Insight Books/Plenum Press.

3   Villena-Mata, D. The Don't Rules in Societal Trauma and Its Healing. Article taken the website version of the magazine: Nonviolent Change Journal, Spring 2002. Retrieved on April 22, 2002 from the world wide web: http://home.earthlink.net/~circlepoint/ncarticle0100.html

4   A resource collection of portrait art depiction of the Castas is, Maria Conception Garcia Saiz's Las Castas Mexicanas: Un género pictórico Americano (The Mexican castas: A genre of American paintings). Milan, Italy, Olivetti,(1989). An internet presentation, Castas Paintings: The Construction and Depiction of Race in Colonial Mexico, can be found at HYPERLINK "http://institutohemisferico.org/archive/studentwork/colony/olson/Casta1.htm" http://institutohemisferico.org/archive/studentwork/colony/olson/Casta1.htm by Christa Johanna Olson, C. J. Accessed 2007.

5   Frank Montalvo's schematic of castes and deeper insights are in the following resources: Danzón and Mexico's Caste System. HYPERLINK "http://www.webcom.com/~intvoice/montalvo3.html . Accessed 2007" http://www.webcom.com/~intvoice/montalvo3.html . Accessed 2007; and Montalvo, F. F. & Codina, G. E. (December 2001). Skin color and Latinos in the United States. Ethnicities, vol. 1, no. 3.

6   Hieronimus, R. (1989). *America's Secret Destiny: Spiritual Vision and the Founding of a Nation.* Rochester, Vermont, Destiny Books.

7   Howard, M. (1989). *The Occult Conspiracy.* New York, MJF Books.

8   *Ibid..* 82

9   Hieronimus, R. (1989). *America's Secret Destiny: Spiritual Vision and the Founding of a Nation.* Rochester, Vermont, Destiny Books.

10 Andrews, W. (1962). Seal, Great, of the United States. *Concise Dictionary of American History.* New York, Charles Scribner's Sons.

11 Hieronimus, R. (1989). *America's Secret Destiny: Spiritual Vision and the Founding of a Nation.* Rochester, Vermont, Destiny Books.; Browder, A. T. (1989). *From The Browder File: 22 Essays on the African American Experience.* Washington, D.C., The Institute of Karmic Guidance.; Browder, A. T. (1992). *Nile Valley Civilization.* Washington, DC, The Institute of Karmic Guidance.

12 Ponessa, J. (1987). Obelisks and the Bible. *Biblical Studies.* Rome, Italy, Pontifical Biblical Institute.

13 Andrews, W. (1962). Seal, Great, of the United States. *Concise Dictionary of American History.* New York, Charles Scribner's Sons.: 860; Browder, A. T. (1992). *Nile Valley Civilization.* Washington, DC, The Institute of Karmic Guidance. 201.

14 Browder, A. T. (1989). *From The Browder File: 22 Essays on the African American Experience.* Washington, D.C., The Institute of Karmic Guidance.; Browder, A. T. (1992). *Nile Valley Civilization.* Washington, DC, The Institute of Karmic Guidance.; Hieronimus, R. (1989). *America's Secret Destiny: Spiritual Vision and the Founding of a Nation.* Rochester, Vermont, Destiny Books.; Lapin, Ð. (1994). Why Jews Have Flourished in America. Crisis: 10-11.

15 (Browder 1989)

16 (Browder 1989; 1992; Hieronimus 1989; Howard 1989; Lapin 1994)

17 Ibid. Browder 1989; Hieronimus 1989.

18 (Wallis 1992)

Forgiveness

Forgiveness is the act of pardoning an offense. Racial forgiveness pardons offenders for their offense and releases the offended party from hostility toward the offender. Mature forgiveness is the result of a reconciled relationship.

Voices of Forgiveness

There were, over the years of my married life, numerous dinners, holidays and special occasions, at my parents-in-laws' home. I dreaded attending these events with our three small children who are now young adults pursuing their own lives and career. I resented conversations that included 'name calling' and 'stereotyping' people. Terms such as 'Wetback' (poor Hispanic/Latino immigrants), 'Chinks' (Asians), 'Sand Nigger' (Arab Americans), etc. were often used. At first, I did not understand, nor had I ever heard, these terms. I asked my husband what they meant. The irony of these episodes is that their three sons married women of color: Chinese, Mexican, and Filipino. My parents-in-laws' (now deceased) attitude and behavior was not only racist but, in my belief, wrong. The stereotyping and name-calling made them feel superior and powerful over certain groups of people whom they found it difficult to respect and appreciate.

Eventually I was able to reconcile these issues with myself and forgive them for their racist and bigoted behavior and attitudes. Of paramount importance to me was the willingness to forgive myself for not speaking out against this type of behavior as much as I should have on these occasions.

— Asian female

~•~

During the time that I was growing up in Southern California back in the 50's and 60's I received a lot of mixed messages about being Japanese American. Dad made it clear that we were American and that the Japanese part of ourselves was something to cover up or downplay. He was obviously reacting to the treatment and shame he felt during World War II when he and his family were loaded on trains and shipped off to internment camps for all people of Japanese ancestry. I grew up feeling that I was somehow better than my other Japanese friends, because I didn't act Japanese. As I grew older I distanced myself more and more from other Japanese Americans. After many more years of seeing the world and understanding how racism warps and distorts both those who sponsor racism and those who are its targets, I have been able to celebrate the part of me that is not American. Only later, as I read about that experience and as I struggled with identity questions in young adulthood, did I begin to understand what had happened to me. And, of course, I resented my father for his role in not lifting up our heritage.

However, a few years ago, something else happened. Dad decided to write his autobiography not too long before he died. I was utterly surprised to learn that his family's home was a center of much of the community's activities. Reading these passages was like a final OK to go back and reclaim more of my past. The healing goes on forever. For Dad it happened almost at the very end. For me, I can go on with the second half of life finally out of the gates of that internment camp.

— Asian male

~•~

A person who was a colleague of mine was trying to make friendly conversation. He told me a racial joke that he thought quite humorous. I was shocked by the joke and told him so. His response was to say that I was too sensitive. From that point on he did not speak about race whenever we encountered each other. Since we did business together, we were often in each other's company. On one occasion, we had a chance to talk about race. I explained why I became angry at his joke, and he explained how he had learned to relate to black people. We had a new appreciation for each other after that. However, I was still holding a grudge, because I thought he really did not understand. I had a hard time forgiving him. Some time after this, I was in a social situation and met his father who proceeded to tell me a racial joke. I grew angry but before I could say anything, his son intervened and explained to his father why this behavior embarrassed and upset him. At that moment I realized that something had changed in my colleague. I was finally able to forgive him for his racial joke.

— Black male

~•~

I once worked at an institution of higher learning. During that time, it had a reputation of admitting African American students, but did not graduate them. Once on board I realized that it was also necessary to retain students and started a program to help them academically. This challenged the status quo and I was treated quite cruelly as a result. I was isolated and left out and accused of being non-collegial. I left shortly thereafter and harbored much anger, resentment and bitterness for years.

The school hired a new dean many years later. He and I became friends and I shared some of my experiences with him. He told me that what happened to me had to happen in order to make an opening for a change to occur at the institution. In that moment,

I learned that it was not about me but something bigger. The pain I suffered lessened it for those students who had come there after me. For the first time I felt like my sacrifices were not in vain. I was able to let go and forgive all of what was done to me in recognition that it was for the greater good.

Note: This has been referred to as the piñata theory. At a party, the child who is blindfolded opens up the piñata by swinging a stick. Once it is opened, all the children run to pick up the candy that spills out. The one who is blindfolded has opened up the piñata, but all the other children reap the benefits of the candy. The blindfolded one seldom gets to reap the fruits of his labor, yet he/she has done something good for the community.

— Black female

~•~

This past year two co-workers were sitting in my office discussing several work topics. I made a comment that to me seemed very innocent, but one of the workers blurted out "there you go again." It seemed that a comment that was neutral to me was culturally insulting to her. It was so insulting that she became very loud and would not let me make a comment. Once she vented, we did discuss what I had said and how it affected her and, she believed, all people of her race.

Although I was reacting with surprise and could not think of what to say at first, I did need to let her vent for as long as she needed. I realized that this person has a whole lifetime of hurt that may boil up and be directed at me. I needed to not only forgive the anger she directed at me but also forgive myself for making comments that are carelessly offensive.

— White male

Personal Examination

Self Aware

How will the act of forgiveness benefit my racial sobriety?

The Forgiveness Stage

Forgiveness is the seventh stage in the recovery from racisms process or it can be viewed as the second stage in racial sobriety. In the forgiveness stage we consider the effects of our racial formation in the family, the community, educational and religious settings. Each one of these places in our lives informed and formed our racial attitudes and behaviors. The importance of forgiveness in racial sobriety was brought home to me by a fellow Ph.D. candidate, William Moore, a psychotherapist. Moore insisted that a Recovery from Racisms™ process for racial sobriety must include the aspect of forgiveness. There must be forgiveness, he argued, in order for people to let go of their hurt, the desire for vengeance to set things right and/or a justice that restores what was lost.

There are several definitions for the word forgiveness. In Greek, the word forgiveness means the release from the bondage of debt and punishment. While in the English, the word forgive means to excuse a fault and to let go of the anger of an offense.[1]

The first person to forgive is oneself for our ignorance and acting on the false beliefs of our racialized self. We need to extend forgiveness also to others in our community of origin. The negative experiences we discover in our "Walk Down Memory Lane" are places where forgiveness is needed. In our "Museum of Racial Memories" there will be those experiences that are healthy and even inspiring events that formed our sense of the dignity of each person. The Racial History Journal is a tool for this reflection, see page 180. The Racial History Journal invites significant racial experiences to come forward and to give insight into how they have affected our lives.

As we journey in our "Museum of Racial Memories" we need to release others from our resentment, hostility and outrage. Family, peers, teachers, preachers and other leaders need to be forgiven. Like ourselves, they too were acting out of a dysfunctional racial-ized identity. As we find a release from our guilt, there is a need to release others who have offended us. We have imprisoned them with the bars of our resentment, hatred or hostility. As we grant pardon to others, we are releasing our minds, hearts and souls from their roles as judge, warden, prison guard and punishing executioner.

The benefit to racial sobriety that the forgiveness stage offers is the release of our negative emotional baggage around racial issues. The act of forgiveness will be one of the most frequently visited stages, because of the racial dysfunction around us. The forgiveness initates a way to release the pent up outrage, righteous indignation, resentment, disappointment and other negative emotions that keep us stuck in our personal guilt and blinded by our self-righteousness toward others. Forgiveness releases these feelings to become new emotional resources in the service of better mental and community health.

Racial forgiveness will take a "fearless moral inventory" of our personal issues and issues outside of ourselves. Four situational encounters will raise issues which call for ongoing acts of forgiveness: Situational encounters with family and community, social transformation working groups, national reconciliation discussions and global reconciliation.

Forgiveness will take an inventory and fearless looking at our issues. The Linn brothers' book *Healing Life's Hurts: Healing Memories through the Five Stages of Forgiveness*[2], would be extremely helpful in this regard. (See page 189.) As with any resource in this area there will often be a real need for someone to assist in facilitating the forgiveness experience. The hurt was not acquired alone but through social interaction. The act of forgiveness, when shared, can be a healing therapy for the human family. Facilitated processes for the act of forgiveness can take many forms, such as, dialogue in peer counseling, religious rituals (confession, penance), cultural ritualizations (sweat lodges for Native Americans), and civic forums (Truth and Reconciliation Commissions) to name a few.

Despite the importance of forgiveness in the recovery process, premature forgiveness is not beneficial. To forgive is to connect with the pain in order to be released from the power of its rage, hostility and resentment. Mature forgiveness is the fruit reaped from the growth of understanding of what happened, how it happened and what is it costing me now. In the light of this understanding, we can see more clearly who we need to forgive, what to forgive, how to forgive, where to forgive and why to forgive. Our hurts are deep. They have been wrapped in personal, social and cultural bandages to protect them from further injury. To unwrap them with the hope of cleaning them and anointing them with a healing salve is not easy. As in family therapy the opening up of the problem is second only to the hurt it causes. Racial dysfunction in the human family is painful to look upon also. Yet the decision to forgive is one of the most powerful acts in the Recovery from Racisms™ process. It is not to be taken lightly with a "premature forgiveness."

Forgiveness requires a maturity born of struggle. Forgiveness takes time. Just as with all the other stages, a person can stand at the door and not enter. Those who do enter the door will find themselves frequent visitors to this address. Each opportunity we take to focus on forgiveness is an occasion for healing of one's racial dysfunction. This healing occurs at many levels. Let us look at three levels of our lives in which this healing can happen: the intrapsychic (psychological/spiritual) level, the interpersonal level and the global level.

Forgiveness in Family/Community

Within ourselves we become aware of the racial dysfunction in which we have been formed and the damage it has caused us in our self-understanding. In Studs Terkel's book *Race: How Blacks and Whites Think and Feel about the American Obsession*, there is an interview with a man who struggles with the three levels of forgiveness in his life. A White Ku Klux Klanner, he saw that his hatred of Blacks gave him a much needed sense of self-esteem. He realized that this was a false pride. It took time for him to realize this and to forgive himself for the ignorance of his naiveté. This act of self-realization brought him to seek forgiveness from his Black brothers and sisters. But he is not ready to forgive the White professional elite who encouraged the racial strife but were too respectable to socially join the Klan.[3] This was a time to forgive self but not to forgive those manipulators who insured their position not only above Blacks but "White trash" in the racial hierarchy by agitation based on the poor Whites need for self-esteem. In this example, E. P. Ellis' conversion prompted him to seek forgiveness from his Black sisters and brothers. At the center of the forgiving act is the conversion to move beyond the racialized self to a bigger picture of humanity. Forgiving self allows for new beginnings.

Forgiveness of family members can give us the needed compassion to understand racial dysfunction as a sickness. Our compassion for our family members who were our first teachers is crucial for our compassion towards our issues and those around us. On the interpersonal level, the ability to forgive often involves the passage of time to distance oneself from the events. Malcolm X, a Black leader in the 1960's, had a conversion experience from hating Whites to seeing everyone as having good and bad within them. As he reviewed his life he could see a need to forgive others due to time, distance and conversion of his mature years. From a safe distance and with the tools of insight and understanding he could look at his family dynamics and see the forces that influenced him. In this understanding of the intrapsychic forces within his father he could realize the interpersonal dynamics of the father's racial dysfunction.

My father was also belligerent toward all the children, except me. The older ones he would beat almost savagely if they broke any of his rules — and he had so many rules it was hard to know them all. Nearly all my whippings came from my mother. I've thought a lot about why. I actually believe that as anti-white as my father was, he was subconsciously so afflicted with the White man's brainwashing of Negroes that he inclined to favor the light ones, and I was his lightest child. Most Negro parents in those days would almost instinctively treat any lighter children better than they did the darker ones. It came directly from the slavery tradition that the "mulatto," because he was visibly nearer to White, was therefore "better".[4]

Not only is forgiveness needed for the child feared, but for the children who were darker and abused. The issues of forgiveness in the Nonwhite community around racial dysfunction that represents the internalization of the white supremacy culture are numerous. The pain of the lighter skin and darker skin is a reality in other communities in the hemisphere. The literature of the Hispanic/Latino countries gives witness to the pain inflicted through internalized racism. The famous St. Martin de Porres of Peru is an example of the shunning of the darker child by his Spanish father who had two children by a mulatto Panamanian wife. St. Martin's dark complexion made him racially unacceptable to serve in civil positions like his father or in the Church of his world.[5] Today the Hispanic/Latino experience continues to act out the shunning of others within their communities due to the hue of their skin. Throughout the world there is a bias against the darker Asians of India, the Philippines and other southeastern countries. Forgiveness within the groups, both White and Nonwhite, as seen in the case of the Klu Klux Klanner with Whites, need to act on forgiveness within their communities of origin.

Social Transformation

Moving from self forgiveness and forgiveness within families and communities of origin, there is forgiveness among those who form intentional communities to promote racial equality and justice. As we seek to make a better world by "making good people better" we will visit the stage of forgiveness often. In the everyday racisms that one encounters forgiveness can only begin with understanding and openness. Without addressing the issues in an open and trusting way healing cannot begin. Nathan Rutstein, the author of *Healing Racism in America,* captures this point in an interracial incident between persons who are committed to working against racism.

The president of the group, a woman of Irish Catholic background, interrupted the black woman: "Look-why drag up what happened in the past. We're making a fresh beginning."

"Look here, time is not what concerns me," the black woman said. "What concerns you?" "Justice." "We're all concerned with justice, or we would not be members of this organization." The black woman's eyes were blazing. "I'm not talking about some pie-in-the-sky justice," she said, poking her chest with a forefinger. "I'm talking about injustices directed at me - by the leadership of this so-called human rights organization."

(The president)"You say I'm a phony do-gooder. I don't remember you saying that when I got you the job you hold now...

...both women, in pain, victims of racism, and unable to work together for a cause they both believed in....[6]

Forgiviness allows both sides to begin again. Without forgiveness we build walls to protect ourselves rather than building bridges to expand ourselves. Building bridges is a benefit of forgiveness that is sorely needed in the antiracism community today. Forgiveness is a resource for building "the beloved community" which Dr. Martin Luther King, Jr. described. The racial baggage that people bring to intentional communitites working for social transformation requires compassion along with intervention. Despite the sincere desire of all parties to construct a racially sober culture within the organization and our society the automatic reflexes of our racial formation can betray the best of intentions. They are the "bad messages playing in our heads." The membership needs to acknowledge that the white supremacy culture in which our racialized self emerged never prepared us to live, learn, play, worship or work together. Our attempts to dismantle racism's 500 year cultural foundations will meet with construction site accidents. Our success depends on how we recover from the setbacks in our group efforts towards racial sobriety. Forgiveness within social transformation organizations is a witness to realizing reconciled relationships in our human family. Through the act of forgiveness these social transformaton groups can become the change they want to see.

National Reconciliation

Forgiveness for the wrongs of our nation against those populations that were considered nonwhite is necessary. Many of the groups that suffered were European immigrant groups who have received redress through their reconciled relationship of white status. But traditional non-European groups have not had redress. Alain Richard traces the horrific genocide and other grave offenses against the indigenous people of the Americas in his book *Roots of Violence in U.S. Culture*. He sees the source of our racial dysfunction rooted in the initial relationship of Europeans and native people. Richard notes that Christopher Columbus wrote in his diary of the Arawak native people: "They would make fine servants...we could subjugate them all and make then do whatever we want." In 1495 Columbus began the slave trade in the New World by enslaving 1500 Arawak of the Caribbean. He took them to Hispaniola (present day Haiti and the Dominican Republic), and initiated the transatlantic slave trade by sending another 500 Arawak to Spain. After 500 years of murder, exploitation and theft, Richard explores the issue of just reparation for the Western Shoshones who had 22 million acres of land in Nevada stolen from them. After decades of arbitration the U.S. still refuses to return the land despite an international treaty. To appease the demand for justice the U.S. government's last offer was to pay for the land which they recognize as legitimately belonging to the Shoshones. However, the government wants to pay the price for the land based on the value of the dollar in 1872! Forgiveness requires a reconciling relationship. Without a relationship of respect and justice, national efforts of redress are a public relations veil over a mountain of horrendous atrocities which continue to this day.

The African presence in the Americas is the second most injured population, second only to the indigenous people in their suffering from the white supremacy of the European population. The oppression of Black populations throughout the hemisphere has differed from that of the native population. The Africans were brought into the hemisphere as valued laborers. Their existence was valued for production and their ability to escape, as with the native enslaved population, was limited. The national discussion of what group is responsible for redress of Black grievances has been ongoing. For most of the 20th century the cry for integration was seen as just and fair. However, the politics of the 60's in the South and the growth of the Black populations in the urban North brought age old grievances and social marginalization to the attention of the nation. In the late 60's there were urban disturbances that had cities on fire and the National Guard called out to calm what was seen as Black rebellion. Marching for justice gave way to cries of Black Power and a sense of Black anger and rage set the stage for a pivotal change of U.S. treatment of its Black citizens.

The changes in society that have led to the integration and greater enfranchisement of the Black community have come to be seen collective as the result of "Affirmative Action" by many pundits, politicians and opinion makers. Whatever one may think however, Affirmative Action was an effort to seek forgiveness from the Black community and to forge a reconciling relationship between Black and White America. It was hoped (proved to be true) that through this act of reconciliation past hurts would be healed. Ira Katznelson gives the historical background of this program for racial reconciliation in his book *When Affirmative Action Was White: An Untold History of Racial Inequality in Twentieth Century America*. He writes that Affirmative Action is today under attack. It is the leading social issue besides the war in Iraq according to social commentators. However, Katznelson argues it is taken out of the context in which it was conceived. President Lyndon Johnson spoke of what we now call Affirmative Action as a bold new social engagement to have the Black American join in the mainstream with the recently enfranchised ethnic Catholics and Jews. Johnson's speech at Howard University, a historic Black university, in 1964 was aimed at acknowledging fault, as it was stated, "the facts of this American failure." Johnson cited, "Thirty-five years ago the rate of unemployment for Negroes and whites was about the same. Tonight, the Negro rate is twice as high." Johnson's hope of creating a reconciling relationship was envisioned as "The Great Society." Affirmative Action was to be a tool to heal the hurts of Black marginalization with a federalized remedy of enfranchisement. Katznelson reasons that a lack of understanding is caused by the fact that the discussion does not include the Affirmative Action programs for Whites that were denied to Blacks. This is the source of a redress for a "Black" Affirmative Action.

Whatever ones opinion on the value, success or future of Affirmative Action as Johnson envisioned it, it has become the most discussed form of social redress. Other Nonwhites, some White minority groups, women and other disadvantaged groups have enjoyed the benefits of the program designed for Black enfranchisement. It is ironic that the greatest number of beneficiaries of Affirmative Action would not be the Black people for whom it was directed toward. However, the nature of forgiveness will require for any group a reconciled relationship to heal the many dysfunctions from which the American family suffers.

Global Reconciliation

In recent years religious groups have asked for forgiveness for the positions they have taken in support of racial dysfunction. The Roman Catholic Church issued a document in 1988 and acknowledged its part in providing a theology to justify the enslavement of the Native Americans and the Africans.[8] Upon the celebration of the 500th anniversary of Columbus' arrival in the Western hemisphere Pope John Paul II apologized to Africans at the Goree Museum in Senegal for the role that the Catholic Church played in the African slave trade. Recently, the National Convention of the Southern Baptists asked forgiveness for the role their Church played in the history of slavery in the Southern areas of the United States. The understanding that pardon is needed opens the way for forgiveness. The payment that the Jewish community is receiving as reparation for the Holocaust speaks to the hope of forgiveness. The reparations being paid in the United States to Native Americans for the grievous history of "Manifest Destiny" and to the Japanese for unjust internment during the Second World War speak to opening the door to forgiveness. The emerging Black Reparations movement in the United States and Africa is demanding the same attention and reparations. However, the hope of forgiveness without the acknowledgment of harm done and the reparation of damages is an empty confession reflecting a shallow remorse.

The stage of forgiveness, on whatever level we encounter it, requires healing. Our hope for a spirit of forgiveness that transforms hurts to healing can only begin when we recognize the offense and acknowledge that our brother or sister has been hurt. This recognition of injury is ongoing and therefore requires an ongoing commitment to justice as an acknowlegement of people's dignity. Silence does not mean consent as we realized with the riots in the 60's. James Baldwin, internationally renowned Black writer, captured the mounting outrage of that time in his 1971 comment.

I had my fill of seeing people come down the gangplank on Wednesday, let us say, speaking not a word of English, and by Friday discovering that I was working for them and they were calling me nigger like everybody else. So that the Italian adventure or even the Jewish adventure, however grim, is distinguished from my own adventure.[9]

Each person and group will have to choose forgivesness on their own terms. The individual seeking racial sobriety will need to be guided by their own lights (religious tradition, life journey, moral development, etc.) to discern the who, what, when, where and why of their act of forgiveness.

Conclusion

Racial forgiveness is an ongoing process in which healing is achieved through reconciled relationships, both past and present. Mature forgiveness is the fruit reaped from an understanding of what happened, why it happened and how it is affecting me now. Racial forgiveness brings to rest the feelings of outrage, hostility and resentment as part of the reconciled relationship.

The stage of forgiveness will be frequently visited as the many levels of our lives call attention to our everyday personal pain and the cry for redress throughout the world.

1 Meier, A. and VanKatwyk, P., Eds. (2001) The Challenge of Forgiveness. "Forgiveness in Post-Affair Couple Therapy." By Martin Rovers. P. 227.

2 Linn, D. and Linn, M. (1978). *Healing Life's Hurts: Healing Memories through the Five Stages of Forgiveness.* New York: Paulist Press.

3 Terkel, S. (1992). *Race: How Blacks and Whites Think and Feel about the American Obsession.* New York, The New Press.

4 Boyd, H. & Allen, R. (1996) Eds. *Brotherman: The Odyssey of Black Men in America-An Anthology.* New York: One World Book Ballantine Books. 80.

5 Garcia-Rivera, A. (1995). *St. Martin de Porres: The "Little Stories" and the Semiotics of Culture.* Maryknoll, New York: Orbis Books.

6 Rutstein, N. (1993). *Healing in America: A Prescription for the Disease.* Springfield, Whitcomp Publishing. 70-73.

7 Katznelson, Ira. (2005) *When Affirmative Action Was White: An Untold History of Racial Inequality in Twentieth Century America.* W.W. Norton & Company: New York. 14-15.

8 *The Church and Racism: Towards a More Fraternal Society.* Pontifical Commission Iustitia et Pax. (1988). Washington, D. C. : United States Catholic Conference. 112.

9 Roediger, D. R. (2005). *Working Toward Whiteness: How America's Immigrants Become White: The Strange Journey from Ellis Island to the Suburbs*, Basic Books. 3.

Witness

Witness is the act of passing on our racial sobriety to others. Witness is becoming the change you want to see at home, in society and the world through a lifestyle of racial sobriety.

Voices of Witness

I was called to the Office of the Dean of the college where I was pursuing graduate studies. My academic advisor at the university and the house mother of the student residence were present at this meeting. The Dean confronted me with a copy of my church bulletin that announced my upcoming marriage. She indicated that the house mother of the dormitory where I resided had informed her that my fiancé was a black man. I asked her what that had to do with the love and respect I felt for him. I told her that I would marry him whether he was black, white, green or with horns. She then said that I was being a traitor to my race and there were going to be consequences. She warned me of the fact that my studies were being sponsored jointly by my country and the United States and she was going to notify both sponsors.

She immediately proceeded to call my country's sponsor at the Ministry of Health and told him what was going on. She also told him the reasons for her opposition. He asked to speak with me and said: "I only have two questions: "Do you love him?" and "Are you pregnant?" After I said Yes to the first and No to the second question, he said, "Then marry the guy and be very happy. Do not worry about anything." Next she called my United States advisor in Washington DC and told him the same story. He told me that if I went through with the wedding I would forfeit the scholarship and have a week to leave this country. He also said that I must see him at his office in Washington DC soon after the wedding. We were married on June 17 and I was in Washington DC on June 19. I left this country on June 25. My husband stayed behind as he had three more semesters to finish his engineering degree.

— Hispanic/Latina female

~•~

I attended a well-known university in my metropolitan Midwest city where I studied for a Masters degree in Social Work. At the end of the semester one of my professors, a white male decided to give me a "B" grade. I was convinced that the paper I had written was an "A" grade. I approached my white professor to inquire why he had given me a B, his answer was simply "I felt you deserved a B. I was not satisfied with his response, so I printed another set of term papers and took it to the Dean (a black female) along with the graded paper. I reported the issue, the Dean made 4 copies of my term paper without my name and gave them to 4 professors to grade, the papers were returned to the Dean with grades between "A+ and A-" The Dean invited the white professor, presented the graded papers to him, and inquired why he gave me a "B." The professor replied that the student was an African and that he does not deserve more than a B, so the dean suggested that the professor re-grade the paper without bias or discrimination. The professor later gave me an A. In this circumstance I witnessed to my self-awareness that African black immigrant students are denied their rightful grades in institutions because of their race. I had to witness to my racial sobriety. Other immigrant students needed my witness in order to demand their rightful grades, regardless of the teacher's racial dysfunction.

— West African immigrant

Personal Examination

Self Aware
How will I witness to my racial sobriety today ? Tomorrow?

The Witness Stage

Witness is the last of the formal eight stages in the Recovery from Racisms™ approach. The emergence of the new self in the place of the racialized self frees us from living under the influence of the "stinking thinking" of racial dysfunction. Witnessing is living out the commitment to see each person as my brother and sister. Witnessing is living S-O-B-E-R: Seeing Others as Being Entitled to Respect in interpersonal relationships; Seeing Others as Being Equally Regarded in society; and globally, Seeing Others as Being our Extended Relations in the human family. This stage is far more than "being" an example of racial sobriety; it is "leading" by example and furthering the healing of the human family.

How do I share the growth and the power of recovery with other people? How do my views affect others? How can I share the benefits of racial sobriety with those around me who are still acting out of the age-old stereotypes? Becoming the change you want to see is the answer to these questions.

It is this witness that gives hope to those who are struggling in the anti-racism movement, and to those who are trampled down by racisms. This witness is seen in the work of the slave abolitionists and Harriett Beecher Stowe's, *Uncle Tom's Cabin*. It is the witness of the Quaker communities that constructed the underground railroad to free slaves fleeing to the North. It is the witness of Dr. Martin Luther King, Jr. and the Civil Rights marchers. It is the witness of the activists who set the prisoner Mandela free to become President Mandela. Witnessing takes many forms as people live their unique testimony as change agents.

Witness as a stage involves testifying to the truth around racial issues. The witness to truth begins with self-awareness and the inner dialogue necessary to sort out the truth. The dialogue of self and the racial incident become a conversation with others as I seek the truth as others might view it. As I am changed by my voice of racial sobriety within, I affect others by my testimony to them.

It is not possible for one definition to capture the meaning of racial witnessing. However, a description of the "ripple effect" of self-awareness in racial witnessing can be seen in five cascading movements. These moments can serve to reveal the development of an act of witness as its "ripples" extend our inner dialogue with the racial event toward the social transformation in the community.

The first moment of self-awareness in witness is that we are present to an event—we are there, in attendance and attuned. We give our attention to the current situation. The first moment of witness is a state of being "in witness of" an experience. That means we are physically present to the reality of an event, be it an act of racism, sexism, ageism, heterosexualism, classism, etc. Our "witness" in the situation can be from various locations. We may be in the situation of our "witness"—with it—or watching from the periphery. We can be an eyewitness with a video camera, or a TV viewer of the evening news. Nonetheless, we are there in our withness. In our witness, we understand the impact and meaning of what we are seeing. This first moment calls for a commitment to stay focused in order to see the event through whether as an observing witness, or as an involved witness. Either way, we make a commitment to be in attendance to the end. We have the options of denial, flight, or rationalization, but we choose to continue "in witness of" the event.

An example of being "in witness of" is the case of Malice Wayne Green. In the city of Detroit, Michigan on Thursday, November 5, 1992, at 10:30 pm, Malice Wayne Green[1] was beaten, kicked and bludgeoned to death by White policemen.

What brought this case to the public was the tape recording of the Emergency Medical Service ambulance driver's question to a supervisor: "What should I do if I witness police brutality/murder?" The driver in the first moment of witness was in witness of a murder.

This brings us to the second moment of witnessing, "witness to." We give testimony to what has happened in order to confirm what we have witnessed. For example, when we observe an incident and call for someone to *verify and testify to* what we have experienced. For social transformation this "witness to" others comes out of a need to process our experience with another's help to clarify and support what we are witnessing. In this moment the witness event becomes a part of our lives and the life of the community in which we give our witness. The event that the ambulance driver witnessed changed his life and the lives of the citizens of Detroit and the surrounding suburbs. Witnessing changes the person and the community at large.

Thirdly, as the witness moments unfold, there is the "witness to accountability." We are directly responsible for our actions and inactions. Whether we are the ambulance driver or the policemen, we are responsible because our actions are a witness to our moral choices. Each person has a set of principles by which he/she lives, an ethical compass that directs moral decision-making. Our witness must be judged by our own vigilant "witness to accountability." We ask ourselves how our sense of justice, compassion and religious persuasion directs our view of an event, and calls forth responsible action. The responsibility of the ambulance driver was to report the incident.

The fourth moment of "witness for," is a movement out of our personal reflection and decision-making to sharing our witness in our community. This conversion from inner reflection to outward action is a "witness for" the victims of racisms and against racial dysfunction in the human family. It is a transformation from being an attentive observer to becoming an actor in the public arena with our testimony. One's "witness for" can include a range of public acts of testimony to give witness to our racial sobriety. The public act of the ambulance driver to alert his supervisor to police brutality was an act of "witness for" justice. The media in covering the story of racial brutality was a "witness for" justice. Whether a private conversation or a public conversation both actions were moments of "witness for" in their testimony to their respective experiences. The importance of one's witness is that it gives testimony in the courtroom of life. We take the stand in our social context and give our testimony - our personal witness. Our personal "witness for" is the voice of the sober self calling forth the community in order to address the racial dysfunction in our midst.

The last of the five moments of witness is that of "witnessing" as an ongoing commitment to give testimony to the truth. This truth of our "witnessing" and its effectiveness must be examined by ourselves and be subject to the judgment of others who share our commitment to racial healing. The ongoing act of "witnessing" to the truth of the human family's dysfunctions around race needs to be updated, renewed and realized in new ways and circumstances. Some of the questions for "witnessing" in the long term include: Is my witnessing morally responsible? Am I doing the right thing in my witnessing? Do I really make a difference in my witnessing? Whether we raise these questions as police officers or ambulance drivers, our actions reflect what we are "witnessing" as a lifestyle in the world.

Also, witnessing to *a* truth is not the same as witnessing to *the* truth. Witnessing against racism can take many forms, and the truth can be found in many circumstances. The truth emerges from a perspective or lens through which we arrange our facts and arguments. This lens gives us a truth for the moment. However, the truth can be elusive. What is true for one moment can begin to shift in the sands of time and circumstances. For instance, in race relations the truth of the struggle has been viewed through various lenses. Some of the lenses of race relations in the last fifty years that were regarded as truths of the movement have been: the integration of the races, civil rights legislation, fair housing, desegragation of schools, self-determination, immigration reform, bilingual education, Japanese American reparations, Native American reparations, economic empowerment, Afrocentrism,

Affirmative Action, etc. Each of these forms of witnessing captured for a moment the truth of the struggle. However, the struggle is more than each one of these efforts. These forms of witnessing to the dignity of all people reflected a particular time and situation in the journey toward truth. In order for witnessing to have integrity and to stay effective, we must witness to *the* truth of the moment. This truth for our witnessing arises out of the clarifying questions that are asked, and the challenge of metaracism to our effective witnessing.

Metaracism is the changing face of racism which like a virus can mutate to overcome the vaccines invented to destroy it. The racism of slavery has ended but it was replaced by the racism of Jim Crow segregation. In order for witnessing to maintain the truthfulness of its testimony, it must examine the metaracism in the culture to discover the "true truth" of its day. Just as the Civil Rights movements advanced the integration goal, the movement asked clarifying questions which advanced the concept of Affirmative Action. Many of the efforts of the past are under attack today by various critics. The act of witnessing must keep up with the forces of metaracism. The truths of racial dysfunction in the 21st century will call forth new actions and strategies of witnessing. Challenges to witnessing today include the racial issues of globalization, immigration, racial profiling, unjust legal sentences, the prison industry, genocide in Africa, and ecological issues of Nonwhite populations. Metaracism can also be seen in the light of the illegal drug industry. In drug and alcohol addiction the amount of the substance over time has to increase to receive the same stimulation. Likewise, as metaracism seeks to maintain the racial caste hierarchy, witnessing efforts will have to double in their effectiveness. It is necessary to clarify the truth of the witnessing moment in order to meet the challenges of the 21st century with integrity and effectiveness.

The example for the five moments of witness that I chose at the opening of this chapter is not the only lens through which to see the stage of witness. A more positive example of the five moments of witness can be seen in Edward Ball's book on race relations in his family, *Slaves in the Family*, which won several book awards.

Ball's work demonstrates the need and the power of witness in overcoming the "Don't Rules" that are a part of his family legacy.

"My father had a little joke that made light of our legacy as a family that had once owned slaves.

"There are five things we don't talk about in the Ball family," *he would say. "Religion, sex, death, money, and the Negroes."* [2]

Ball researched his family through generations and their ownership of four thousand slaves in the history of the family's Charleston, South Carolina plantations. He followed up his research with interviews of the descendents of the Ball family's slaves. He went so far as to go to Sierra Leone in West Africa where the majority of the slaves had their origin, and interviewed the African sellers of the slaves.

The witness value of Ball's work is beyond measure. Through his witness to the unity of the human family and its sharing the responsibility of racial dysfunction, one can see that the five moments of witnessing can also be a positive healing experience. The truth of Ball's witnessing has begun a conversation that defies the "Don't Rules" and provides a model of the "Do Rules" of racial sobriety for this American family and the global family.

Conclusion

Witness is the goal and the summit of Racial Sobriety™. The act of witness gives testimony to the triumph of the human spirit over oppression. Efforts such as those of the White and Nonwhite abolitionists in the United States were successful in their intervention on the nation's dysfunction because of their active witness. Witness is always successful for the person giving it, because it makes real their commitment to racial sobriety. Witnessing does not fail. It can only grow more successful and insightful with perseverance and time.

In any recovery process, program or movement, there is an obligation for the person who has benefited from the healing journey to pass it on to others. Witnessing is the profound act that shares one's racial sobriety in order to free us from racial dysfunction and brings together the human family.

1 "Fatal beating by police outrages city leaders" (Chief to seek charges for some of the 7 cops involved). *The Detroit News and Free Press*. November 7, 1992. Front page.

2 Ball, E. (2001). *Slaves in the Family*. New York: Ballantine Books.

Where Do I Go From Here?

Voices Across the Globe, Generations and Gender

Robert Manuel, the president of the parish council, was seated at a table with a group of visitors to the church from out of town. A family from Ohio had come to Detroit, Michigan to visit the associate pastor and brought along a high school foreign exchange student from Argentina. The young Argentinean exclaimed gleefully, "I can't believe I am sitting here with all these Negroes!" She was excited and happy. The rest of the people at the table, who were Black and White Americans, were taken by surprise with her comment. She went on to explain that her parents would not allow her into the capital city of Buenos Aires because of the dangers of coming in contact with Black people. She was excited to be in the presence of Black people. She commented on how pleasant and friendly all the Negroes were.

Robert Manuel, who was sitting at the head of the table, asked, "Would you like to see our tails?" This comment drew everyone's attention to him. We had no idea what he was referring to, but the young Argentinean did. She responded excitedly, "Yes, can I see your tails?" We looked at her with disbelief, both Black and White. Robert, who was in his 60's, told us that in World War II in Europe the White soldiers told the European women that the Black soldiers were animals with tails. He went on to say that there were situations that he knew of in which European women would sleep with Black soldiers. They made sure to keep the Black soldier with them until midnight to see them turn into animals and see their tails come out. He thought that if the young woman's parents had told her how bad Blacks in Argentina were they might have mentioned that Blacks also have tails. Evidently, he was right. He went on to explain that Blacks did not have tails.

This encounter between the White Latin American exchange student and the Black World War II veteran changed everyone's day that afternoon. Each time I play this scene in my mind from time to time I realize another insight about the global reality of today's racism. I also realize that racism will continue from one generation to the next through family formation. How similar the views of the young lady were to members in the suburbs of many American cities. Here at the other end of the hemisphere is a reflection of the city and the suburbs of Detroit where there is a media portrayal of Blacks as dangerous and animal-like. Racism is not limited to this hemisphere it is also exported through American military personnel to other countries. The haunting revelation in that afternoon encounter was how the culture of white supremacy is a net that catches everyone up in it. Robert in his 60's had suffered the stereotype of being presented as animal-like in Europe while fighting for his country. Two generations later this young not-yet 20 year old shattered the assumption that race relations were better in South America and that young people do not have the racism present in older people. It does show, however, the global and intergenerational dysfunction that is a part of daily life on the planet.

-Black male

Where do we go from here?

At the end of the workshops presented by Certified Facilitators of Racial Sobriety™ there is usually the question, "Now what do I do?" The question is one that arises from a newly acquired awareness of living under the influence of racial dysfunction. There is a desire to intervene on the stinking thinking of racisms and the role it plays in the culture of white supremacy. This last chapter is to give direction to the reader who has a passion to become the change they want to see. Hopefully, you will find your

"Journey toward Racial Sobriety" as you answer your desire to know, "Where do we go from here?"

The Journey toward Racial Sobriety

To begin one's growth in racial sobriety is to make a commitment to live on the self-aware level of the racialized self. It is most comfortable to be unaware of our racialized self because our awareness requires a response to the racial others in our lives. It is a response that is often unpleasant and full of stressful emotional promptings. This is also true for the self aware level which calls us to responsibility by reflecting on what is happening within ourselves in order to advance in our racial sobriety. The benefit of living on the self-aware level is the growth of our human personality as we reach a greater capacity to be fully functioning human beings. Our capacity for functioning as full human beings is rewarded by growing self esteem within ourselves and social confidence in our interactions with others.

When accepting the challenge of recovery from racisms the individual can experience anxiety from within. The pillar of our fear is the main support for the gate of anxiety that blocks our Journey to Racial Sobriety. (See page 192.) Our personal struggle within ourselves is represented by our feeling of anxiety, which is fueled by our fears, ignorance and guilt. Pushing open the gate of our anxiety takes the power of the "Do Rules" in which we break the taboos of talking about race, explore our feelings and trust ourselves to find the best strategies to move forward on our journey. Talking ourselves sober is the everyday challenge of racial sobriety. The dialogue of the racialized self and the sober self is ongoing. Our feelings and the information they bring to us are the heart of the conversation within us between the racialized self and the sober self. On the Journey to Racial Sobriety the racialized self and the sober self are conversation partners. The way our feelings inform our lives is described in *Emotional Intelligence at Work* by Hendrie Weisinger. "It is important to keep in mind that it is your own thoughts, bodily changes and behaviors that drive your emotional responses, not someone else's actions or an external event."[1]

In the recovery process, our emotions often surprise us in the form of "automatic thoughts" as responses to racial encounters. Weisinger's insights give direction on how to grow from our emotional distress by seeing when and how we respond. The emotions associated with racial encounters require "inner dialogues" or "internal conversations" in Weisinger's terms in order to learn how we can take control of our responses. The discovery of new perspectives which replace our stinking thinking with an appropriate response is the product of our internal conversations. Our feelings provide "instructive statements" for the sober self which replace the statements of racialized self. Our voice of racial sobriety engages our feelings to follow the "Do Rules" as we discover our way toward racial sobriety. Under the direction of the sober self our behavior follows a new script as we become the change we want to see.

The other pillar on the Journey To Racial Sobriety supports the gate marked "Resistance." The pillar of strength for this gate is entitled "Digression." We will face resistance on the journey from those against our progress as well as those who journey with us. The object of digression is to keep us from the path. We are continually threatened by the forces of white supremacy and its hidden hands of economic and political power. However, resistance is the nature of life. It is through the power of physical resistance that we are able to stand up, to inhale and exhale, to live, love and laugh. Our resistance is never futile. Our lives from our mothers' labor to give us birth to the last throes of death are the products of the force of resistance. Our resistance to the forces of racial dysfunction in our society is a sign of our mental and emotional health. Our resistance gives birth to a culture of racial sobriety.

Resistance on the Journey

Our strides in self awareness are intensified and strengthened through support from others. This support can be informal through encouraging conversation with like minds. Formal support groups made up of friends, peers, professional associates, etc. can greatly enhance and advance our capacity for growth. (See page 194.)

The Healing Circle as a support group process provides a sense of New Family Formation in which we can share the benefits of seeing each person as our brother and sister. Participation in Healing Circles benefits everyone in the group and provides insights into the journey which are not available when working alone. However, the journey is not to depend on others. To do so would make us co-dependent on others decisions to engage in recovery work. Our racial sobriety is enhanced by others; it is never to be co-dependent on others recovery.

Groups seeking racial sobriety will encounter resistance from within the group itself. Resistance is often seen in the act of digression, which is choosing to leave the path and discuss a topic other than racism. Three common forms of digression found within workshops and Healing Circles are: MIA, hijackers and heroes/sheroes. The resistance of the MIA, "missing in action," is to ask the question "Why are we here?" This form of resistance challenges the group to halt the discussion in order to convince the person of the importance of the subject and the process. This is a common digression and needs to be addressed immediately. It is not the role of the members of the Healing Circle to convince someone of their need to recover. It is after gaining the desire to recover that one enters a Healing Circle. The group is a Healing Circle for racial dysfunctions and if the person is an MIA they have wandered into the wrong place.

The second common form of digression is that of "hijacking," that is taking the Healing Circle from its destination of racial sobriety. The most common efforts at hijacking the Healing Circle redirect the issues of racism to various other social dysfunctions. All of these issues are indeed worthy of consideration; however, the "hijacking" of a Healing Circle does not respect the group's goal as well as the worthiness of other social illnesses. Whatever the motivation of those seeking to hijack the Healing Circle, they have made a decision not to address the topic of their issues and racial dysfunction. The Healing Circle is to stay focused on the goal of racial sobriety.

The third common dynamic is that of heroism by members of the group. These "heroes and sheroes" stop the sharing process because they are uncomfortable with the group's honesty and openness and what it will require of them. This response is prompted by their desire to save the group from a perceived danger of too much openness. Superman or Superwoman feels empowered to save the group when in reality they want to save themselves from a fear of exposure of their own issues or the failure to share with integrity as others have done. By acting for others they believe that they have the high moral ground in their disruptive behavior and receive a sense of heroism in the process. The group is harmed by this false heroism as they are held hostages to one person's fear of being racially sober. When this is allowed to go unchallenged the hero or shero sabotages their recovery and the members of the Healing Circle. These three challenges of resistance in groups have to be confronted immediately in order to maintain the integrity of the Healing Circle experience. To assist the groups in maintaining a healthy Healing Circle, a protocol is provided in the appendix, see page 194.

Historical Cultural Resistance

Beyond the resistance within ourselves and the Healing Circle we face a culture of resistance. As we become the change we want to see in race relations we will be challenged constantly with resistance from the culture of racial dysfunction that surrounds us. Until the focus of immigration and September 11th emerged in the national conversation around race there was a growing sense of appreciation and tolerance of racial and cultural differences. The focus on the growing number of Nonwhite immigrants has changed the tone of the media conversation from appreciation of cultural differences and tolerance to insensitivity and hostility. The sources of hostility are seen as a backlash from previous White immigrants and Nonwhites who feel their white privilege or social and political gains are in jeopardy. Despite the Civil Rights Movement and the legislation to address discrimination and acts of prejudice we still live in a highly racialized culture. There is not a cry over European immigration or Cuban immigration but it becomes an issue when Nonwhites approach our "For Whites Only" borders as in the case of the Haitians and the Hispanic/Latino communities. There is a cultural bedrock of racial dysfunction throughout this hemisphere against those deemed nonwhite.

The historical roots of racial dysfunction originate in the adoption of the racial castes constructed in New Spain, present day Mexico. The Catholics of Latin America and the Caribbean had slavery as an integral part of their colonization of non-Catholics from their Roman cultural foundation. Slavery and Christianity in the Americas would become synonymous with the adoption of racial castes by the Anglo-Saxon Protestant culture of North America as early as 1667. The Anglo Protestant paradigm for racial difference was found in their biblical worldview, (see page 199.) In their interpretation the English were the Chosen People of God entering the Promised Land of North America. In this scenario their "Manifest Destiny"[4] under God, the Native Americans were regarded as the biblical Canaanites who were to be cleansed from the land by whatever means. African slavery was also theologized by extending the curse on Canaan to his father Ham. The biblical understanding of the many peoples of the world was found in the Table of Nations in the Book of Genesis. National, ethnic and racial differences were attributed to Noah whose three sons represent the three branches of the family tree of humankind. Ham was considered the father of African people, Shem was the father of Asian people and Japheth was considered the father of Europeans. Because of Ham's sin against his father Noah, his son Canaan was cursed to serve his brothers: "Cursed be Canaan! The lowest of slaves shall he be to his brothers." (Genesis 9:25 *New American Bible*). The curse to be the slave of his brothers was not placed upon the descendents of Ham but on the descendents of Canaan. Since slaves were forbidden to read they would not be able to refute this scenario of divine destiny in which the White man was destined to rule and the African to serve. The native American population would be the victim of state sponsored genocide and made as nonhumans in this biblical paradigm in which they were guilty of living on someone else's "Promised Land."

The second lens recognizes the transition from Christian supremacy culture centered on baptized White people to supremacy based on simply whiteness without the inclusion of baptism. In the "White Anglo Lens" of the 1800's Catholic immigrants were not considered white because they were not white Anglo Saxon Protestants. Because the increasing number of Catholic immigrants referred to as "ethnics" the borders were closed . The racial categories of the "White/Nonwhite culture" were: White, Indian, Colored and Ethnic. Today we live in a "Pan-American Culture" which denotes the expanding power of the originating European colonization of the Spanish. Presently we live and interact in white supremacy culture throughout the hemisphere. The cultural interpretation of racial interactions varies and forms a plurality of cultures. In some cultural settings races are separated by law while others form their culture around being marginalized by the inequalities of economics, education and housing. In the midst of this pluricultural reality there are cultural circles where there is racial integration and healthy interaction. Though the lens of our cultural and racial dysfunction developed over time they co-exist today. The daily journey through our society, whether personally or through media reports, we encounter the pluricultural lenses in which people see one another in our racialized world.

The Present Cultural Challenges

Fifty years ago on April 15, 1947, Jackie Robinson integrated major league baseball. There is no doubt that the American family has made progress. But we are also challenged by another observance. It is the 40th anniversary of the assassination of Dr. Marin Martin Luther King on April 4, 1968 which set off a series of urban riots throughout the nation. A review of the legacy of the 1960's and 1970's is underway. Works such as *The Black Power Movement: Rethinking the Civil Rights –Black Power Era* by Joseph Peniel are capturing this historical moment, clarifying its social gains and charting new directions. Authors highlight the emergence of Black consciousness raising, grass roots community development, black self-determination, black capitalism and many other concepts. Writers and social commentators like in Amos N. Wilson's *Blueprint for Black Power: A Moral, Political, and Economic Imperative for the Twenty-First Century* also have a forward looking motivation for their assessment of the late twentieth century. Beyond the movements generated within the Black community are the cultural responses of the society to Black demands in such legal enactments as the War on Poverty and Affirmative Action. Employment opportunities and educational opportunities for Nonwhites flourished at the time. However, the 40th anniversary of movement is marked by a series of reversals of these actions which will undermine the gains made by Blacks, other Nonwhites and Women. Derrick Bell, a legal scholar and social analyst, has analyzed the weakness of legal redress in the civil rights gains. As a lawyer for hundreds of school desegregation cases, Bell describes in *Silent Covenants: Brown v. Board of Education and the Unfulfilled Hopes for Racial Reform,* the cultural impediment for Nonwhite advancement. Bell defines the "silent covenant" as a legal understanding by policymakers to "stand ready to modify or even withdraw the reforms" when the white status quo is affected.[6] He notes that this "silent covenant" originated with the protection of slavery in the Constitution and was reinforced after Reconstruction in the Hayes-Tilden compromise that led to the lynching of thousands of Blacks to re-establish white supremacy throughout the south.[7] As U.S. society revisits the urban riots of the 60's the assessments of the event and their effect on our present political and social realities will provide a catalyst for a sorely needed discussion in the American family.[8]

Writers, scholars and commentators in the White community are also reviewing the annals of the American family's racial journal. Paul Clemens challenges us to "do the right thing"[9] in his work *Made in Detroit: A South of 8 Mile Memoir.* He reflects on the racial changes in Detroit, Michigan from the viewpoint of being a white family in a city that was to become eighty percent Black. He narrates his everyday experience in the midst of the growing Black population and the flight of the White population. The scholar Scott L. Malcomson makes a chilling observation about the reverse white flight represented in the form of urban regentrification in his multiracial history *One Drop of Blood: The American Misadventure of Race.*

"The neighborhood they improve, however old and previously

peopled, will be new, in the same way that America was new and empty when the English arrived and when John Locke saw that a land ruled by an Indian king was not really his land because he had not "Reason to guide him," and so had not fully used the land, and so should be displaced by more gifted people.

...White and nonwhite will still be members of one divided family... they will again go to racially separate graves in the mistaken belief that that is freedom."[10]

Malcomson's prediction is based on the choices that we make to ignore our family history of racial dysfunction. Our cultural denial of racial realities leaves us thinking of progress in terms of race relations rather than living through a cultural cycle seen in the post Civil War Reconstruction being repeated in the 21st century.

The Pluricultural Challenge

There are many voices writing on race relations and they represent the plurality of racialized cultures that have formed as a result of the segregation of racial groups by the elites in the dominant white supremacy culture. The cultural reality of these social arrangements has formed pluricultural circles in society and within our lives. Pluricultural describes the awareness of how each person or group sees the world from the perspective of the cultural "frame" they place around it while at the same time being aware that they exist in the cultural "frame" of other people and groups. A pluricultural perspective takes into account that we participate in multiple "frames" at the same time in our everyday interactions with others. This awareness becomes more evident with the increasing number of cultural frames encountered and negotiated in a given lifestyle. The plurality of cultures which we frame and in which we are framed are without limit. Some of the cultural frames include the following: urban, suburban, White, Black, Hispanic/Latino, Asian, gendered, middle class, working class, religious affiliation and ethnic identification with racial groups. We find ourselves "framed" by those living in reference to these cultural forces just as we "frame" them from our cultural centers. The pluricultural perspective has a heightened awareness of the power of white supremacy culture as the most powerful tool in our culture to "frame" others because it is the culture that provides the terms and language for the conversation on race, diversity and multicultural issues.

Racial sobriety is challenged by the pluricultural frame imposed by white supremacy culture. The division of people as White, Nonwhite, People of Color, etc. provides a plurality of group identifications maintained by elite circles within social institutions resulting in "institutional racism." Through the social network of elites the plurality of cultural setting is regulated in housing, employment, education, policing, etc. The most powerful tool of the elite in the pluricultural reality is the regulation of the conversation on race, gender and class so as to construct and communicate the social value of one's identity in relationship to everyone else's identity. In the western hemisphere the cultural elite exercise power over the social construction and the valuing process in three major areas: race, gender and class. Just as the GPS (Global Positioning System) provides a map for traveling by car, plane or boat by the coordination of a position by three different satellites, in the same manner the elements of one's social identity can be located and mapped out. The three social satellites to be coordinated are race, gender and class. They are society's three satellites which form its own "GPS," that is "Global Positioning in Society" for locating our position in terms of the road to enfranchisement through various social terrains.

The pluricultural challenge of framing others while at the some time being the object of their framing is increasing incidents of racial dysfunction. Since September 11, 2001 the growth of "Islamophobia" has become a focus of national anxiety along with Hispanic/Latino immigration. The group interaction dynamics of racial dysfunction around Islamophobia was the catalyst for the first national meeting of Arab leaders with U.S. government officials on incidents of attacks in 2006. The Arab American leader and university professor M. A. Muqtedar Khan chaired the program. He observed, "Recognizing that anti-Americanism and Islamophobia feed each other, the panelists called for simultaneously addressing both prejudices."[11] The U.S. position was not to talk about the increasing incidents of "Islamophobia" because it would only deepen the divide. This position represents the time worn avoidance of reality by imposing the "Don't Talk Rule." We cannot address the issue without the conversation. As we continue to identify groups as "the other" and not part of the American family we make them targets for our cultural aggression.

New challenges posed by increasing pluricultural issues not only arise from events outside of our society but from within as well. The striking down of laws against interracial marriage in the mid 1960's in over 30 states and the advancement in the integration of the races have produced "interracial marriages" and "multiracial children." This relatively new phenomena is changing how more and more people are looking at the race issue as a "family issue" for Nonwhites and Whites as each group finds that blood relatives have varied shades of skin. We learn how to find our way within a community.But when one belongs to two racial communities the demands are taxing. Navigating the seas of racial dysfunction is changeable and perilous as Gregory Howard Williams narrates in *Life on the Color Line: The True Story of a White Boy Who Discovered He Was Black.* Williams narrates his life in the white and nonwhite community and what happens when the pretense ends.[12] Another voice that speaks of this experience is James Mc Bride who narrates the experience of growing up in the Black community with a Jewish mother in *The Color of Water: A Black Man's Tribute to His White Mother.* He reflects the need to see beyond color to find allies in the racial battlefields of everyday reality.

"Mommy was for anything involving the improvement of our education and condition, and while she would be quick to point out that "some Jews can't stand you," she also, in her crazy contradictory way, communicated the sense to us that if we were lucky enough to come across the right Jew in our travels --- a teacher, a copy, a merchant --- he would be kinder than other white folks. She never spoke about Jewish people as white. She spoke about them as Jews, which made them somehow different."[13]

As we move toward the future with increasing pluricultural

encounters society is faced with the inclusion of new populations to our already centuries old racial hierarchy. What future lies ahead for our pluricultural present?

Future Cultural Resistance

The history of cultural resistance to seeing each person as our brother or sister is the core reality of our present social relations. It is our history of racial casting that can become at times of economic stress and social uncertainty our frightening future. The significance of the global connection between the naming of the indigenous people as Indians of India and the construction of a racial caste has yet to be fully explored. Gonzalo Aguirre Beltran is the renowned pioneer of the history of the racial castes of Mexico. In his work *La Poblacion Negra de Mexico: Estudio Etnohistorico (The Black Population of Mexico: An Ethnic Study)* Beltran makes reference to the caste of India as the adopted social structure for New Spain or Mexico.[14] But the 500 year construction of the racial caste hierarchy demonstrates the power of the caste system in the human global family. The enduring power of this sociopathic institution of racial caste is the fundamental social phenomena in the culture of the western hemisphere. Both its affects and effects have yet to be fully appreciated in the history of American republics and human history.

The future of race relations is presented by Professor Eduardo Bonilla-Silva, a sociologist and expert in the historical dynamics of racial casting in the North and South American cultures. Bonilla sees the U.S. taking a page from the notebook of Hispanic racial supremacy as it reconstructs race relations that incorporate the growing Latino/Hispanic population. In the second edition of his groundbreaking work *Racism Without Racists: Color-Blind Racism an the Persistence of Racial Inequality in the United States*, Bonilla predicts that the Mexican castes are being resurrected and the socio-pathology of this type of racial dysfunction will engulf the 21st century North American cultural life. A quarter century ago the media described the appearance of the increasing Hispanic/Latino population as the "Browning of America." The color "brown" was chosen as a place between the racial spectrum of "white" and "black."[15] In this reconfiguration of color casting the browns of U.S. society would fit in between the whites and the blacks. Bonilla sees in this reshuffling of the race cards what he calls the "Latin Americanization" of U.S. race relations. He proposes the emerging new reconfiguration in which the Anglo racial castes and the originating Mexican castes will include the new global immigrants. Bonilla calls his forecast a "Preliminary Map of Triracial Order in the USA."[16] (See table on next page.)

This prediction of the reconstruction of the racial caste hierarchy rather than destroying it presents a sad commentary on the mental health of our society. As much as we would like to refute such a prediction the media daily reports the emerging social interactions that support the evidence of our racially casted reality. Reports ranging from the unfair police stops of Nonwhites to random murders of our citizens due to the racial identification ascribed to them. However the construction of a racial caste hierarchy is a concerted act of an elite within a society. Just as the conquistadors of Spain established racial castes 500 years ago in present day Haiti and the Dominican Republic, we have the same elite forces in our society re-gentrifying social interaction with the precision of a GPS device.

The future of the U.S. in the "Browning of America" metaphor held within it the social notion that the Hispanic population would relieve the black and white division in society. However, the offer to exchange a "mestizo" or mixed blood racial identity for a race card to pass as "Honorary Whites" could change the "Browning of America" to the "Whitening of America." This would repeat the historical encounter of Catholic and Asian immigrants with the Anglo Saxon Protestant culture of the 19th and 20th century in which they struggled to escape their nonwhite status in the pursuit of the promise of whiteness. This pursuit of whiteness inevitably fuels the fires of racial turmoil throughout society as each racial group struggles against the other.[17] The groups are pitted against one another in a daily contest to gain enfranchisement for themselves and their offspring, just as their competitors will fight to maintain their privileges as a legacy for their children.

Rather than racial casting disappearing into our shameful past history this racial dysfunction could become the prideful boast of many in our foreseeable future.

Preliminary Map of
Triracial Order in the USA

"Whites"
Whites
New whites (Russians, Albanians, etc.)
Assimilated white Latinos
Some multiracials
Assimilated (urban) Native Americans
A few Asian-origin people

"Honorary Whites"
Light-skinned Latinos
Japanese Americans
Korean Americans
Asian Indians
Chinese Americans
Middle Eastern Americans
Most multiracials

"Collective Black"
Vietnamese Americans
Filipino Americans
Hmong Americans
Laotian Americans
Dark-skinned Latinos
Blacks
New West Indian and African immigrants
Reservation-bound Native Americans

Leadership for a Culture of Racial Sobriety

Leadership in race relations for the 21st century needs to engage the historical struggle of promoting the dignity of each person in our society. The social sobriety requires that we see our society as a family in which we are brothers and sisters: Seeing others as being entitled to respect. Leadership in constructing a culture of racial sobriety will call for leaders to emerge within our racial, cultural and religious groups. The leaders need not be seen as White or Nonwhite leadership but as leadership within a community, on the job, in the organization or in the society in general. These leaders will need to network with their brothers and sisters who are promoting racial sobriety throughout our pluricultural society. These leaders will form an elite circle to offset the forces that are promoting racial dysfunction at every level of our society, which is the reason why racially sober leadership needs to surface at every level of our society.

It is not about Nonwhite leadership or White leadership. It is about racially sober leadership. Take for example the football team referred to as "The Fighting Irish" though most of the players are not Irish. In order to win in the world of college athletics a decision was made to re-engage their paradigm of who could be a member of the "Irish" team. It is the same reengagement that is needed to have a leadership team that can win for the forces of racial sobriety. Crucial to the construction of a culture of racial sobriety is leadership from the White community. Just as the Nonwhite community needs Black roles models, Hispanic/Latino role models, Asian role models, etc, we need to have White role models for White people. This country is a White country and there will be no success without White role models to show the White community what racial sobriety looks like. The idea of progress without White role models is unimaginable and literally impossible.

As we celebrate Jackie Robinson integrating baseball we cannot do that without honoring Wesley Branch Rickey, the white baseball executive who owned the team. Rickey was not satisfied to integrate baseball with Blacks, he also brought the first Hispanic into national league baseball, Roberto Clemente. Wesley Branch Rickey was a White role model and brought racial sobriety to his professional world. He was referred to as "The Mahatma" for his leadership in social change.

We also observe the 50th anniversary of the desegregation of the Armed Services by President Harry S. Trumann in Executive Order 9981 on July 26,1948. President Truman created in his executive action the most integrated institution of American life, the Armed Services. This achievement has not been matched in any other institution including education and religion. President Truman was a White role model. Kathrine Drexel of Philadelphia was a millionairess who founded a religious order of women dedicated to the education of Black and Native American children. She used her wealth to support over 250 White women teaching in 10 school across the nation. She is a White role model. In a pluricultural society White role model are needed for White and Nonwhite people.

White role model in a society that expects Nonwhite to lead in race relations is a new paradigm for many. Beverly Daniel Tatum as an educator and author in the area of race relations captures the cultural challenge of leaders in the White community finding their voice of racial sobriety in the American family. Tatum has her students keep a journal in her class which she reviews. She highlights one of those entries that spotlight the cultural challenge of leadership in the White community.

"Yes, there is fear," one White woman writes, "the fear of speaking is overwhelming.

I do not feel, for me, that it is the fear of rejection from people of my race, but anger and disdain from people of color: the ones who I am fighting for." In my response to this woman's comment, I explain that she needs to fight for herself, not for people of color.

After all, she has been damaged by the cycle of racism, too, though perhaps this is less obvious. If she speaks because she needs to speak perhaps then it would be less important whether the people of color are appreciative of her comments. She seems to understand my comments, but the fear remains."[18]

The struggle to find one's voice in the midst of racial dysfunction within our own community of origin and in the midst of other racial communities is the core of the FIG complex. The fear-ignorance-guilt dynamics hold hostage those who would seek racial sobriety for themselves and provide leadership for the construction of a culture of racial sobriety. White and Nonwhite mentors, educators, pastors, counselors are key to the development of White voices in a predominantly white civilization. The silence of white voices of racial sobriety is deafening. The leadership in the Nonwhite community today requires a review of not only the Civil Rights era and the Black Power movement but to engage the plurality of nonwhite cultures in our midst. The Black movement became the model for other racial struggle, gender struggles, age struggles (The Gray Panthers) and class struggles here and abroad. The creative passion for the dignity of everyone was at the core of the movement. Today we need an inclusive movement that includes the human struggle of the American family. It will have to acknowledge that the great American tragedy is the Native American and all the indigenous people in the indigenous people of the western hemisphere. The emergence of the American family as one integrated whole is making itself into print. To see larger picture Iris Chang in *The Chinese in America* sets the racial oppression of the Chinese in the context of Blacks and Native Americans. Chang cites:

"In California, the state legislature at one time offered bounty hunters a fee for each Indian scalp turned in. Eventually murder, hunger, heartbreak, and disease had their desired effect. In 1790 there were almost four million American Indians, but by 1844, fewer than thirty thousand remained, a much more manageable Inconvenience for the white man."[19]

Nonwhite leadership requires seeking everyone as victims of racial dysfunction. Nonwhite leadership includes enlarging the struggle and connecting the historical progress of role of racial hierarchy across borders. The Hispanic/Latino presence continually informs that history of the hemisphere as centered in Mexico, formerly New Spain. In New Spain the 1646 census is over 35,000 African slaves and more than 16,000 people of African descent.[20] The exploration of the African presence in Mexico is produces many new works and projects. The dynamics of naming difference and determining its historical origin and present impact on racial stratificiation is creating a body of literature for pluricultural scholarship. *Blacks in Colonial Vera Cruz (Mexico)* by Patrick J. Carroll explores the ongoing dynamics of the "Afro-castas"[21] in the history of Mexico. *Neither Enemies Nor Friends:Latinos, Blacks, Afro-Latinos* edited by Anani Dzidzienyo and Suzanne Oboler is the groundbreaking work of fifteen scholars examining new relationships between ethnic and racial identity, or the lack of relationships depending on how the frame in which a group's identity is viewed.[22] The pluricultural identity emerges from the intersections of race, ethnicity and region.

In the white leadership model in which 15% of any community are leaders and the rest are followers is an insight that leadership in every aspect of our society is a capacity of the few and not the many. W. E. B. Du Bois, the Black intellectual of the 20th century also felt there was in the Black community a percentage who had the capacity for leadership in race relations. He called this group "the Talented Tenth." No matter the percentage the reality that leadership skills in every community is a gift or capacity that is not found in everyone but evident in a few. The elite of the various institutions are the social actors who "do the heavy lifting" for its community. An example from the sports world is that of a city's team. In the arena or the stadium there are thousands of fans cheering, but in reality it is the team that is playing. However, when the team wins, the city wins. The players represent the elite athletes working in behalf of their city; the players do the heavy lifting for thousands sitting in the stands or their couches at home. It is the players that have the capacity for leadership in this endeavor. So too with race relations, there are those in our communities that have the capacity for leadership in race relations, they do the heavy lifting for their teams. On the side of human development are the players of racial sobriety; while on the "other" side are those elites who use racial dysfunction to score the points for their projects of economic development and human impoverishment in the world. Each player does the heavy lifting on behalf of their side.

The nature of leadership capacity and the power of elitist circles challenge everyone to reflect on the role of White leadership in race relations. In the rhetoric and strategies of the Black power movement of the 60's, the role of White people was to be in the background and to support of Black leadership. This line in the sand of the racial politics has diminished a capacity of leadership in a nation that is White. In terms of leadership just as Nonwhite people needed to develop new skills of leadership, Whites now need to develop White role models of leadership for the White community as we construct a new culture in which we form a family paradigm over institutional models of social progress. The crucial development for our time will be White leadership with a capacity to construct a culture of racial sobriety in a culture of white supremacy.

Conclusion

Racial Sobriety™ is a tool for those seeking a healing process for themselves and for the construction of a culture of racial sobriety within our homes, communities, institutions and society. Though Racial Sobriety focuses on the racisms in midst, it is also a template to address "sexisms," "classisms" and "ageisms." I stress the plural forms of these words to underscore the multiple dimensions of each of these dysfunctions in the human family. For instance, racisms affect Nonwhites, Whites and Intermediates, but they share the struggle to maintain the status quo of racial dysfunction as they suffer because of it. Likewise, the dysfunctional influence of sexisms (subordination of women, homophobia, patriarchy, etc.) victimizes our lives. The human dilemma leaves no one unharmed or free from our shared family dysfunctions. George Curry, the journalist and publisher, speaking at a conference used the paradigm of recovery to describe people who are getting things done in the midst of dysfunctional culture.

He said, "Some people are drunks and some are alcoholics. The alcoholics go to meetings. The drunks don't."[23] Likewise, we suffer with racial dysfunction, but some are working on their issues and others are not.

Racial sobriety's healing paradigm requires a commitment to seeing humanity as a family in the global context. Seeing the world as our family challenges the globalization phenomena that sees human beings as resources for capital and labor to exploit, to steal from, to dominate and exterminate. We need new ways to see our in our differences our common humanity. Gregory Orfalea offers a paradigm that moves beyond "the melting pot" in *The Arab American: A History*. He reflects on the meaning of a quilt made by his grandmother Thatee.

"The quilt is stitched of triangles of material, and the triangles overlap each other... A slit of darkness, triangles of dark brown and black and maroon ... It's the whole cycle of a human being's life stitched in discards ... All Thatee's pain was gathered in cloth: her two infant brothers breathing their last orange breaths in Shreen; her husband picking the last orange apricot, mildewed at the middle; ... the orange start of a day with all the children gone ... Thatee, I hear you. In these gorgeous remnants, you made a life that would last."[24]

The American family's racial, cultural and religious elements create a pluricultural quilt when seen through the lens of our shared lives together. Matilda Awad's (Thatee) quilt hangs in the entrance of the Arab American Museum opened in 2005 in Dearborn, Michigan. A changing nation in search for a transition into a global community can realizes its potential from the culture that changed our civilization from Roman numerals to the Arabic numerals in which we construct our lives today. The global community and the U.S. in particular, represented as a quilt of colors offers an alternative from a posture of tolerance until the "un meltable ethnics" are assimilated, to a posture of appreciation of the beauty of every hue in our humanity, the music of diverse languages and the richness of religious expressions in which the American family has wrapped itself within.

To the question, "Where one goes from here?" The answer is,

Straight ahead!"

Take advantage of opportunities to share the racial sobrity with others. Sponsor an introduction to the approach with a discussion of this book. For groups that wish to have such a program with a trained facilitator, go to the Racial Sobriety webpage: www.racialsobriety.org. An introductory program can be promoted in May, which is Racial Sobriety Month. There are other months that various racial groups have during the year for example: Black History Month, Hispanic/Latino History Month, Native American History Month, Asian American, etc. When presenting a context for struggle in the world today note the role of racial supremacy in the Katrina response disaster, in the genocide of Dafur and the poverty and suffering in the only Black republic in the hemisphere, Haiti. The need for intervention on behalf of our brothers and sisters can be overwhelming if we accept responsibility for it. We are not responsible for it but we are called to respond to it. We are also called to honor those who engage in making a difference. For example, the role of the media in racial supremacy is evident. However, we are called to honor those who use it to educate and inform with the same passion as we criticize those who use it to perpetuate racial dysfunction. As the social and cultural forces around us challenge our racial sobriety, we struggle along with others to bring sanity to the human family. You and I are to encourage one another as we become the change we want to see.

[1] Weisinger, H. (1998). *Emotional Intelligence at Work.* Jossy-Bass, San Francisco. 29-36.

[2] Maxwell, J. F. (975). *Slavery and the Catholic Church.* London: Brown & Son (Ringwood) Ltd. 10 and 86.

[3] Russell, K., Wilson, M., Hall, R. (1992). *The Color Complex: The Politics of Skin Color Among African Americans.* New York: Harcourt Brace Jovanovich, Publishers. 10.

[4] Horsman, R. (1981). *Race and Manifest Destiny: The Origins of American Anglo-Saxonism.* Cambridge, MA., Harvard University Press.

[5] The Book of Genesis 9:25. *The New American Bible.* (1986). New York: Catholic Book Publishing Company. 12.

[6] Bell, D. (2004). *Silent Covenants: Brown v. Board of Education and the unfulfilled hopes of racial reform.* Oxford University Press, New York. 5

[7] Ibid. 47.

[8] A wide spectrum of Black American voices reflecting on the last 40 years also inclu de: Joseph, P.E., Ed. (2006). *The Black Power Movement-Re-thinking the Civil Rights and Black Power Era.* New York, Routledge; Cose, E (1993). *The Rage of a Privileged Class: Why are middle-class Blacks angry? Why should America care?* New York, HarperCollins; Williams, J (2006) *Enough: The Phony Leaders, Dead End Movements, Culture of Failure That Are Undermining Black American-And What We Can Do About it.* New York, Crown Publishers.

[9] Clemens, P. (2005). *Made in Detroit: A south of 8 Mile memoir.* New York: Doubleday. 241.

[10] Malcomson, S. L. (2000). *One Drop of Blood: The American Misadventure of Race.* New York, Farrar Straus Giroux. 490.

[11] "Government looks at Islamophobia." By M. A. Muqtedar Khan. The Arab American. December 23, 2006-January 5, 2007. Vol. 22, Issue 1089/1090. 13

[12] Williams, G. H. (1996). *Life on the Colorline: The true story of a white boy who discovered he was black.* New York, Plume.

[13] McBride, J. (1996). *The Color of Water: A Black Man's Tribute to His White Mother.* New York, Riverhead Books. 66.

[14] Beltan, A. (1989) 3rd Edition. *La Poblacion Negra de Mexico: Estudio Etnohistoric.* Unniversidad Vera Cruzana Instituto Nacional Indgenista Goberno Del Estato De Veracruz. Fondo De Cultura Economica: Mexico, D. F. 292.

[15] This phrase was coined by Richard Rodriguez, a Mexican American writer. Rodriquez is also the author of *Brown: The Last Discovery of America in 2002.*

[16] Bonilla-Silva, E. (2006) 2nd Ed. Racism Without Racists: Color-Blind Racism and the Persistence of Racial Inequality in the United States. New York: Rowman & Littlefield Publishers, Inc. 180.

[17] Williams, C. Ed. (1997). *Building Bridges in Black and Brown: The dialogue between the African American and Hispanic/Latino Communities.* Detroit, Michigan, Building Bridges in Black and Brown.

[18] Tatum, B. D. (1997). *"Why Are All the Black Kids Sitting Together in the Cafeteria?": And Other Conversations About Race.* New York, NY, Basic Books. 194.

[19] Chang, I. (2003). *The Chinese American.* New York: Viking Books. 25.

[20] Bennett, H., L. (2003). *Africans in Colonial Mexico: Absolutism, Christianity, an Afro-Creole Consciousness,* 1570-1640. Indianapolis, IN: Indiana University Press.

[21] Carroll, P. J. (2001). *Blacks in Colonial Veracruz: Race, ethnicity and regional development.* 2nd Edition. Austin, Texas: University of Texas Press. 141-3.

[22] Dzidzienyo, A. and Oboler, S. Eds. (2005). *Neither Enemies Nor Friends: Latinos, Blacks, Afro-Latinos.* New York: Palgrave Macmillan. 121.

[23] George E.Curry, National Newspaper Publishers Association –Editor in Chief, speaking at the Forum on "Future of Black Men" sponsored by the NAACP in Desdin, Florida on December 12, 2006. Aired on C-Span January 8, 2007 at 10:57 PM EST.

[24] Orfale a. G. (2006). *The Arab Americans: A History.* Northhampton, Massachusetts: Interlink Publishing Group, Inc. (Olive Branch Press). 434-5.

New Family Formation Covenant

1) I am here to grow stronger in my recovery from racisms.

2) I am here to find support for my recovery and to give support by discovering alternative ways of thinking and acting.

3) I am not here to tell others how to deal with the racisms in their lives because such a response would only limit the attention I give my own situation. I gain the insights and courage to recover as I witness the struggle of others through active and engaged listening.

4) The highest goal of the Focal Support Group is MY recovery. The deeper I can go in my journey to recovery, the deeper the Healing Circle can follow, support and affirm my new self and the new self in others.

The "Check-In" Exercise[1]

After the Introductory Session to the Racial Sobriety™ program each session begins with the "Check-In" exercise. Through this exercise the individual's work and the group's work are reviewed in the Healing Circle.

Individual Work

I) The facilitator/leader/host begins the session by initiating a sharing process focused on each member's treatment plan for recovery from racisms which was presented in the previous session.

2) Each member shares his/her treatment plan and reviews how his/her efforts addressed their goals.

Group Work

3) New Family Formation Housekeeping

a) The facilitator/leader/host asks the members of the group how they feel about the level of acceptance by everyone within the Healing Circle they have formed.

• Does anyone think he/she is being slighted in the group? If so, why?

• Does anyone think another member is being slighted in the group? If so, why?

• How does each member in the group describe the level of acceptance in the Healing Circle?

b) Is there a feeling of belonging in the Healing Circle among the members?

• How is this sense of belonging fostered, observed by the members, appreciated by the participants?

c) Do we value each other's journey towards recovery in how we listen to others?

• Do we value one another in our responding to each other's story?

4) Continue with the session's focus from the Stages of Recovery Cycle. (See page 194 at 22 minutes into the session.)

1 This procedure is adapted from Ellen Pence and Michael Paymar's, *Education Groups for Men Who Batter.* Springer Publishing Company: New York, NY. 1993.

Appendix A

"Death and Dying" Overlays for Recovery from Racism Stages

Stages	Kubler-Ross *Facing Death and Dying*	Linn Brothers *Healing Life's Hurts*	Recovery from Everyday Racisms Racial Sobriety
Denial	"I don't ever admit I will die."	"I don't admit I was ever hurt in life."	"I don't admit that my everyday actions reproduce and support the white supremacy culture."
Anger	"I blame others for letting death hurt and destroy me."	"I blame others for hurting and destroying me."	"I strike out at others who identify my internalization of the culture and/or I strike out at others who make me a victim of their racisms."
Bargaining	"I set up conditions to be fulfilled before I'm ready to die."	"I set up conditions to be fulfilled before I'm ready to forgive."	"I try to fulfill the conditions that will give me 'social innocence' in regard to racisms."
Depression	"I blame myself for letting death destroy me."	"I blame myself for letting hurt destroy me."	"My inward focused anger represents my powerlessness to make a difference to affect the white supremacy culture."
Acceptance	"I am at peace with the knowledge that I am going to die."	"l look forward to growth from my hurt."	"I accept the responsibility for my own recovery from racial dysfunction within myself and the racisms that surround me."

Appendix B

Appendix C

Appendix D

Appendix E

Peruvian Table

Man	Woman	Offspring (Male)	Mixture
White	Negra	Mulato blanco	1/2 white & 1/2black
White	Mulata Blanca	Mulato morisco	3/4 white & 1/4 black
Negro	India	Mulato pardo	1/2 black & 1/2 Indian
Mulato pardo	India	Mulato lobo ("wolf")	1/4 black & 3/4 Indian
Mestizo	Mulata parda	Mestizo pardo ("coyote")	1/4 black & 1/4 white & 1/2 Indian
Mestizo	Negra	Mestizo prieto	1/2 black & 1/4 white & 1/4 Indian

Appendix F

Journey to Racial Sobriety

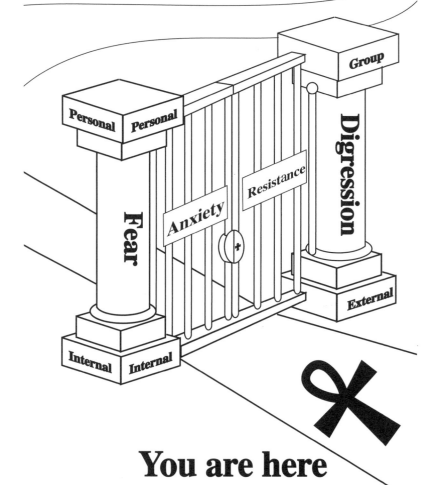

You are here

Appendix G

The Racial History Journal

The Racial History Journal is an exercise to demonstrate that everyone has a history of racial encounters in his/her socialization process. The exercise is divided into various periods in one's journey through life. Each period has provided experiences of racial formation for the individual through events, situations, choices, etc.

Age	Significant Experience
Primary	
Teens	
20s	
30s	
40s	
50s	
60s	
70s	
80s	

90 Minute Small Group Sharing Session

This format can be used in conjunction with the chapters of the book for small groups that wish to share the journey toward racial sobriety.

Minutes   Process

:00   Welcome one another with a friendly gesture

:04   The New Family Formation Covenant recited (See page 187.)

:07   Check-In exercise (See page 187.)

:22   The leader will facilitate a discussion on the chapter of a particular stage of Racial Sobriety. Participants respond with their comments and insights.

:40   The group shares their struggle for recovery reflecting on the stage they discussed in the previous session.

:65   Members take time to personally reflect on the treatment plan for the coming week based on the "Personal Examination" of the chapter and the group's discussion of the chapter.

:70   Members share their goals of treatment for the coming week.

:80   Closing comments from the leader.

:85   Adjournment and parting greetings.

Appendix H
The Stages of Recovery

Appendix I

The 16 Racial Castes of Colonial Mexico

1. Spanish man with Indigenous woman
Mestizo

5. Mulatto with Spanish woman
Morisca

6. Morisco man with Spanish woman
Chino

7. Chino man with Indigenous woman
Salta atrás

11. Albarazado man with Black woman
Canbujo

12. Canbujo man with Indigenous woman **Sanbaigo**

13. Sanbaigo man with Indigenous woman
Calpamulatto

2. Mestizo with
Spanish woman
Castizo

3. Castizo man with
Spanish woman
Spanish

4. Spanish man
with Mora Black
woman **Mulatto**

8. Salta atrás man
with Mulatto woman
Lobo

9. Lobo man with
Chino woman
Gibaro

10. Gibaro man
with Mulatto woman
Albarazado

14. Calpamulatto
man with
Canbuja woman
Tente en el Aire

15. Tente en el Aire
man with
Black woman
No te entiendo

16. No te entiendo
man with Indigenous
Woman **Torna atras**

Appendix J

Socio-Economic Pyramid of Racial Castes

Appendix K

Appendix L
The Sociotext

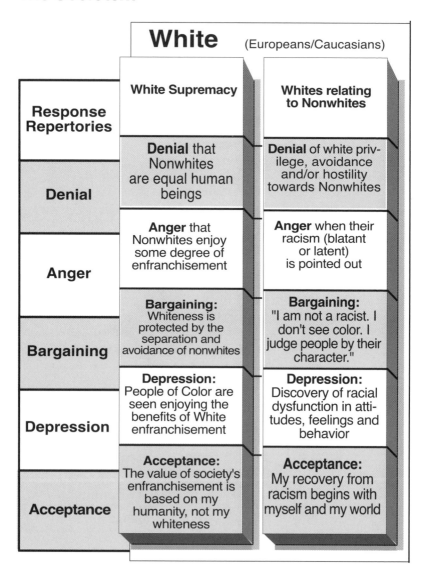

White (Europeans/Caucasians)		
Response Repertories	**White Supremacy**	**Whites relating to Nonwhites**
Denial	**Denial** that Nonwhites are equal human beings	**Denial** of white privilege, avoidance and/or hostility towards Nonwhites
Anger	**Anger** that Nonwhites enjoy some degree of enfranchisement	**Anger** when their racism (blatant or latent) is pointed out
Bargaining	**Bargaining:** Whiteness is protected by the separation and avoidance of nonwhites	**Bargaining:** "I am not a racist. I don't see color. I judge people by their character."
Depression	**Depression:** People of Color are seen enjoying the benefits of White enfranchisement	**Depression:** Discovery of racial dysfunction in attitudes, feelings and behavior
Acceptance	**Acceptance:** The value of society's enfranchisement is based on my humanity, not my whiteness	**Acceptance:** My recovery from racism begins with myself and my world

Nonwhite (People of Color)

Nonwhites relating to Whites	Nonwhite Supremacy	Colorists/ Intermediates
Denial of the effects of racism in their life	**Denial** that Whites are people, both good and bad	**Denial** of their nonwhiteness
Anger at the realization that racism has circumscribed and impacted their life from birth	**Anger** that Nonwhites do not see what White society is perpetrating	**Anger** when their humanity is denied or confined based on nonwhiteness
Bargaining: "I am not like the rest of the Nonwhite race," i.e. Oreo (Black), Apple (Native), Coconut (Hispanic), Banana (Asian)	**Bargaining:** Separation from white control of Nonwhite community and psyche	**Bargaining:** To escape the oppression - I am not nonwhite, only partially so
Depression: No guarantee of equal treatment, kept in their place	**Depression:** Realizing that Nonwhites are inter-connected with White society	**Depression:** Society does not let one escape their nonwhite status
Acceptance: Acceptance of operating in a hostile society	**Acceptance:** Nonwhites are part of society and deserve to be enfranchised	**Acceptance:** To recover my self-esteem based on my person, not my degree of - whiteness

The Purpose and Use
of the Sociotext

The Sociotext for Recovery from Racisms™ presents an arrangement of responses from various communities of origin within the white supremacy culture. The responses from these communities are ordered according to their relationship to the "death and dying" stages of Dr. Elisabeth Kubler-Ross. The intent of the sociotext is to suggest that the person seeking racial sobriety will have to adopt a "death and dying" paradigm to do their recovery from racisms work. The person will have to "die" to the racialized self that was formed in their community of origin and is perpetuated in their reference community and intentional communities.

The sociotext itself is a schema that reflects reading the great currents of racial dysfunction in the nation/family of the United States. In the context of a white supremacy culture, the two great divisions of the nation/family are the white and nonwhite populations. To these great historical divisions, today we are challenged to include the large number of recent Americans or immigrants who are considered nonwhite. Within this social context, the sociotext was constructed to read the social texts of racial dysfunction in terms of the two major communities of origin, "White" and "Nonwhite." Recognizing the power structure in a white supremacy culture, the "White" communities of origin are the "in-group" which is enfranchised with privilege. In such an arrangement "Nonwhite" communities of origin represent the "out-group" which is disenfranchised from privilege due to the forces of white supremacy. To give recognition to other observable behaviors, there is a representation of the "Colorist/Intermediate" communities of origin that challenge the traditional "Black and White" paradigm of race relations. The "Colorists" represent those Nonwhites (Asian, Black, Hispanic/Latino, Native American and recent immigrants) who seek to "pass" as White people although their ancestral gene pool, according to the racial laws of the United States would not allow whiteness to be conferred on them.[1] The "Colorists" community representation is linked to the "Intermediates" who are recent immigrants. The term "Intermediates" reflects the "in-between status" of immigrant groups, they are in between white and nonwhite status until their racial caste location is assigned. This group often resists being classified into the existing racial caste of the United States system and seeks to identify with their nation of origin. However, "Intermediates" are by force of the racialization process challenged to see themselves within the terms provided by the United States census and the common social practice of seeing people in regard to their position in the racial caste hierarchy. This is most clearly seen in the growing request of Hispanic/Latinos to specify within their communities whether they prefer being considered a Black Hispanic or White Hispanic. [2]

As Marger noted in *Race and Ethnic Relations: American and Global Perspective*.

...race is one of the most misunderstood, misused, and often dangerous concepts of the modern world. It is not applied dispassionately by laypeople or even, to a great extent, by social scientists. Rather, it arouses emotions such as hate, fear, anger, loyalty, pride, and prejudice. It has also been used to justify some of the most appalling injustices and mistreatments of humans by other humans. [3]

This nation has made race a paramount issue for its "Manifest Destiny" in the nation's westward expansion. The historical foundations are set deep in the American holocaust of the Native Americans, the enslavement of African people and exclusionary immigration laws against Asians.[4] These traumas in the cultural history of the nation/family have resulted in the present racial caste hierarchy. The cultural history of the nation/family is the source of its racial dysfunction as a nation and a global power. This nation/family history has to be faced when seeking to personally and culturally recover from racisms.

The Recovery from Racisms™ paradigm uses a metaphor that compares the nation to a dysfunctional family. The nation/family idea is that a country functions like a large family and any illness affects every member of the family. Racial dysfunction is an illness in the American family which is inclusive of White families and Nonwhite families. Immigrants as new Americans are socialized and racialized into the nation/family's racial dysfunction upon their arrival at our shores and borders. This racialized formation has enveloped Africans, Arabs, Asians, Europeans, Hispanics, and other immigrants. Unfortunately for both those newly arriving and for long time residents this racialization will continue to increase the breadth and depth of racial dysfunctional in the culture to the peril of all involved.

The sociotext presents a schema of communities in which the recovering person will find their re-engagement work. The three specific communities of re-engagement are: the community of origin, the reference community and the intentional community. Most of our social interactions are found in one of these three communities. Our childhood formation is represented by the community of origin. The reference community is found in the workplace and professional associations within the larger society. And there are also the intentional communities of voluntary associations, religious affiliation, etc.

In the White and Nonwhite communities as general headings it must be acknowledged that other groups exist, though not in great numbers. Nevertheless they are present in our society and influence the culture. For example, two groups that are not mentioned in the sociotext are the "new abolitionists" who represent those Whites desiring to leave the White race[5] to join the human race, and those Nonwhitess who hate other Nonwhites.[6] In the first case of the "new abolitionist" community their appearance is new and the literature is in a state of formation. In the case of those Nonwhites who hate other Nonwhites, although it is a distinct community within society, they comprise only a small population overall.

The sociotext in the Recovery from Racisms™ process is a tool for personal work in the journey toward racial sobriety. A person who is seeking to have sober racial interactions can become overwhelmed by the racial dysfunction around them. The sociotext helps to identify the fact that there are various responses that will be present in a multitude of daily situations. Each person will need to be handled appropriately by a recovering person. The sociotext is to help locate the problem of racial dysfunction in the culture rather than in an individual. In most cases the individual is acting out of a cultural script provided by the racialized self. But a caution is necessary. Many people have a paradigm of changing the world but not themselves. Recovery from Racisms™, like any recovery program, is directed towards self-healing before assisting others. It is the old story of finding a splinter in another's eye while overlooking the log in our own eye. Therefore, a caution is issued in regard to using the sociotext to address another person's recovery instead of addressing one's own.

The warning against using the sociotext to project a rescovery path onto others is illustrated by the following example of how people see themselves. Without getting into a person's head how could one judge the recovery work an individual would seek for themselves. Clara E. Rodriguez is the author of the book *Changing Race: Latinos, the Census, and the History of Ethnicity in the United States*. She shares her experience of one family's choice of racial association.

A Dominican student of mine told me that each of her and her husband's children claimed a different identity. So they had one black child, one white child, and one Dominican child. Each of the children had different friends and tastes. Many variables contribute to and interact with the racialization process to determine how individuals decide on their group affiliation. Generation, phenotype, previous and current class position, and the size and accessibility of one's cultural or national-origin group, as well as the relative size of other groups, all affect how individual Latinos identify themselves.[7]

The sociotext is best used for identifying one's own reality. Any projection onto other actors in a social setting can at best be doubtful. As seen from this story, the caution of using the sociotext for other than personal work is discouraged. This is especially true in consideration of the Colorist/Intermediate groups but it is also true for any of the groups within our society. There is a story told about people who live their lives through other people's eyes. In the substance abuse recovery community this person is called "a co-dependent." A co-dependent is defined as a person who has someone else's life flashing in front of them when they are drowing in a lake. Likewise, imagining another person's recovery makes you a co-dependent to their racial dysfunction.

The value of one's insight into another's motivation is limited given all the forces that would have to be considered. For example, the issue of "passing as white" for members of the United States community has a negative meaning in both the White and the Nonwhite communities. However, new immigrants to this country would not immediately appreciate the act of "passing" as White, Black or Hispanic due to their lack of history with race relations and the social context for "passing." Their viewpoints in terms of their own racial formation in this country are under construction by various forces in our white supremacy culture. Rodriquez notes later in her book on race and Latinos that, when comparing other recent immigrants with the Hispanic/Latino population, there is a great resistance in accepting the American racial caste hierarchy in place of their self identification when they arrived in the United States. Also, Asians interpreted race as a question of "national origin" as did Haitians in Miami, and Latinos from such countries as Puerto Rico , the Dominican Republic and Honduras.[8]

The sociotext is presented to demonstrate that everyone in the society has issues of racial dysfunction to address. The place to start to address those issues is within one's self. There is enough work there for a lifetime of recovery. This does not take away from the value of the overview of the behaviors that can be observed in the various communities of origin. It does help us to locate ourselves in the larger picture of our society and communities to begin the personal transformation that leads ultimately to social transformation.

1 Lopez, I. (1995). "The Social Construction of Race." *Critical Race Theory: The Cutting Edge* Ed. Richard Delgado. Philadelphia: Temple University Press.

2 Hacker, A. (1992). *Two Nations*. NY, NY: Scribners.

3 Marger, M. (1991). *Race and Ethnic Relations: American and Global Perspectives*. Second Edition. Belmont, CA.: Wadsworth Publishing, 1991. 18-19.

4 Horsman, R. (1981). *Race and Manifest Destiny: The Origins of American of Racial Anglo-Saxonism*. Cambridge, MA: Harvard University Press.

5 "Treason to Whiteness is Loyalty to Humanity: An Interview with Noel Ignatiev of Race Traitor Magazine.": *Utne Reader.* November/December 1 994.

6 Fanon, F. (1952). *Black Skin White Mask*. Grove Press: New York, 1967 (original in French, 1952).

7 Rodriquez, C. (2000). *Changing Race: Latinos, the Census, and the History of Ethnicity in the United States*. New York: New York University Press. 19-20.

8 Ibid. 151.

About the author

Fr. Clarence Williams, CPPS, Ph.D.

Fr. Clarence Williams, CPPS, PhD is the founder of the Institute for Recovery from Racisms™. Fr. Williams has a doctorate in Education and Cultural Communication from the Union Institute and University in Cincinnati, Ohio. The Institute for Recovery from Racisms is dedicated to training facilitators and designing programs to promote Racial Sobriety™. He has produced three national teleconferences on racism. The "live" interactive programs have reached over 11,000 participants. The Rev. Dr. Williams is the author of *Recovery from Everyday Racisms* (1998) and *Racial Sobriety: A Journey from Hurts to Healing* (2002). He has given workshops and presentations on racism throughout the nation as well as in Europe, Africa and South America. His works are available in Spanish and Portugese.

In the area of Cultural Communication, Fr. Williams is the co-founder of Building Bridges a program that presents workshops on how to "bridge" between racial and cultural groups. He is the editor of the book, *People of the Pyramids: The Dialogue Between the African American and the Hispanic/Latino Communities* (1997)." The "Building Bridges Process" was developed through four national conferences on building bridges between the African American and the Hispanic/Latino communities from 1992 to 1997. He presents his program regularly for groups such as General Motors World Headquarters and Catholic Charities USA.